CONTENTS

WHAT EVERY PARENT NEEDS TO KNOW ABOUT...

EMERGING SEXUAL TRENDS AMONG OUR YOUTH

TONJA H. KRAUTTER

PUBLISHED BY FASTPENCIL, INC.

I dedicate this book to my two boys, Tyler and Brody Pearson. I strongly believe that God blessed me with two sons for a reason. It is my hope as a parent that I will continue to be granted the wisdom, strength, guidance, and support necessary to successfully raise them. It is my hope that they will follow in their father's footsteps to be respectful and kind; thoughtful and sincere; and loving and caring human beings in our society. This would be my greatest life achievement.

ح

Acknowledgements

I am a Practicing Clinical Psychologist who finds great meaning in helping others. I feel honored and privileged to work in the mental health field. In addition, I am a mother who finds great meaning in raising two precious children. Both my family and my career are priorities in my life. I feel blessed to have created a balance between them.

Identification and understanding of the emerging sexual trends among our youth can leave a family feeling frustrated, frightened, confused, and defeated. My greatest hope in writing this book is to provide knowledge to all families who are currently raising pre-teen or teenage children in our society today. We are witnessing first hand a dramatic cultural shift in regards to sex and sexual relationships. By acknowledging this shift, we are able to gain a better understanding of the complexities involved and offered the opportunity to help our children in both positive and healthy ways not only in regards to sex, but in all areas of their lives.

I would like to acknowledge the contributions of several people, without whom, I would not have completed this book.

To the many people who supported me in my efforts and convinced me that this book was a must read for parents who are raising pre-teens and teenagers in society today: Andrea Ancha, Shelly Swan, Anthony Atwell, Fawn Powers, Gale Uhl, Judith Siegel, Larry Gibson (R.I.P.), James Cosse (R.I.P.), Carole Brennan, Maritza Jensen, Tiffany DeSantis, Ruth Welsch, Sara Gray, Sara Pearson, Valerie Waagen, Melissa Sorci, Janice O'Deegan, Andrea Lee, Juana Olsen, Nicole Memoli, and Heidi and Al Krautter.

To my incredible husband and soul mate, Jason, whose constant encouragement and reassurance during the development of this book was invaluable. To my two amazing sons, Tyler and Brody, who had to give up several hours of "mommy time" in order to allow for the completion of this book.

To my incredible pre-teen and teenage patients who have been consistently open and honest with me about their experiences in today's society with sex and sexual relationships. You are the source of my inspiration for writing this book. The readers ultimately have you to thank for their acquired information and knowledge.

To my good friend, Steve O'Deegan, for his hard work and commitment to the finalized product. Thank you all!

1

INTRODUCTION

There is no denying that things change in society on a continual basis throughout time.

I think most people would agree that an evolving society is not necessarily a bad thing. In fact many changes are viewed as highly positive. However, this is not the case for all shifts in our society. Probably one of the most frightening changes we have seen over the past few decades are those which have to do with sex among our youth. There has been a rapid shift from predominantly "prude-like" behaviors to promiscuity among both boys and girls. Parents are completely horrified when they learn that their children, who have barely hit puberty, are engaging in sexual activities that not too long ago were reserved for only married couples.

Our society has moved from viewing girls as 'treasures' to viewing them as 'sex objects.' Many boys are seen as disrespectful, impatient, and crude when interacting with girls, which is different from in the past. It was not too long ago that boys would be excited simply to hold a girls hand. 'Stealing a kiss' would cause a boy's heart to beat out of his chest with nervousness and exhilaration. Boys would not even contemplate stepping past those boundaries because quite frankly, they knew they would be shot. Literally, a girl's father could and often would take a shotgun to any boy who placed hands on his unwed daughter. Therefore, boys tended to follow an unspoken process to begin building a relationship with a girl that they were interested in.

First, the boy would ask the girl's father for permission to "court" his daughter. Do our teens even know what that word means? The boy might bring a girl some flowers or take her on a walk. They would then progress to going on a date, perhaps to a community dance. Taking someone out on a date and getting to know them seems to be passé. It is amazing to me how many teens have never been on an actual date, but have had sex with multiple partners. This is quite a change from a community dance where the couple might hold hands or have their first kiss. The final step in courting was when the boy would ask the girls father for permission to marry her. If the father agreed, then the two would marry and begin building their own life and family together.

Girls no longer look to their parents for permission to spend time with boys and boys rarely ask for it. Both boys and girls take it upon themselves to make decisions about who they will spend time with and what sexual activities they will engage in with this person. Perhaps this would not be viewed as negative if it was not happening at such a young age.

We have a new sexual movement occuring in our culture. It is important that we become educated about it. The sexual trends that are emerging in our society are alarming to say the least. However, perhaps what is even more alarming is the fact that most adults are unaware that they exist. This book was written with the purpose to educate parents. Identification of the trends and why we are seeing them emerge in our society will be covered in the next two chapters of this book. How to avoid the emergence of these trends and how to deal with them will be covered in chapter 4 and chapter 5. These two chapters (4 and 5) are particularly important because they will provide answers to the many commonly asked questions by parents regarding what to do if their minor child.

It is my hope that with a more thorough understanding of the complexities of our culture's emerging sexual trends, we will be better equipped to work together as a society toward prevention and intervention. "It takes a community to raise a child" is one of my favorite quotes. "Our children are our future, let them lead the way" is another. Right now, their leadership on this topic is frightening in the way that they are leading each other. Therefore, it needs to become our job as parents to lead them. Our children deserve to be guided, taught, and mentored in a positive and healthy ways so that they can pass down what they have learned to the next generation. The topic of sex is something that many parents have difficulty discussing with their children. After reading this book, I hope that all parents feel more confident and comfortable engaging in these conversations with their kids for years to come.

2

WHAT ARE THE EMERGING SEXUAL TRENDS AMONG OUR YOUTH?

The first emerging sexual trend among our youth is that sex is starting at a younger age.

As mentioned earlier, most individuals in the past waited until marriage to have sex with their partner. This clearly is no longer the case. It is not uncommon for both High Schoolers and Middle Schoolers to be engaging in sexual activity. That is right, even middle school children are sexually active. Some school districts in varying states are so overwhelmed with the increase in young teen and pre-teen sex that they are taking matters into their own hands by handing out birth control on their school campuses.

The main concern for most school districts is teen pregnancy prevention. However, this type of decision brings on a huge debate. In fact, a few years ago (2007) we witnessed a national firestorm when a Portland, Maine school board decided to allow birth control pills to be distributed to girls as young as 11, without parental consent. The country was in an uproar. Points were made that middle schooler's are having sex and therefore, girls must be protected from pregnancy. Individuals for the idea noted that since condoms are often freely handed out at school, it is not that big of a jump to hand out birth control pills to sexually active students. Others disagreed. Individuals against the idea noted that most school districts around the country require parents to give permission to the school nurse in order for their children to take over-the-counter medications like Tylenol. Several schools even require a doctor's note for cough drops and sunscreen. Therefore, providing a prescription drug to minors without having to inform the parent seemed outrageous and completely hypocritical.

It is estimated that more than one third of ninth-graders have had sex with someone else. Not only is sex starting at a younger age, but the progression of intimacy is moving faster among our youth. This trend is an important one to consider especially for parents. What it means for parents is that if your child has a new boyfriend or girlfriend, you will need to think about talking to him or her sooner rather than later about sex and intimacy. It used to be that if a pre-teen or teen got a boyfriend or girlfriend, intimacy would progress slowly and gradually through a span of several months or years. What would start off with a kiss only several months later might turn into fondling and then several months after that might turn into something more sexually intimate. It often took years to reach the time for a couple to consider having sex.

Consideration of 'sex before marriage' was seen as the "big sexual movement" in the 1960's. We are now witnessing a whole new sexual movement among our youth. It is not uncommon for teens to talk about having sex with their boyfriend or girlfriend within the first month of being together. In addition, it is not uncommon for sex to occur when two people are not even in a committed relationship. Sex is happening younger, faster, and with multiple partners.

The combination of these factors (sex happening younger, faster, and with multiple partners) illustrates the next common trend that we are seeing in our society today among our youth. Sex is much more casual. Our teens do not believe that they need to have a boyfriend or girlfriend in order to have sex. Many of our teens are engaging in what is called "friends with benefits" also known as "f-buddies." F-buddies does not stand for "friendly buddies," "funny buddies" or "fantastic buddies." It stands for "fuck buddies." Excuse the language, but since your children may refer to it as this, it is important to note and understand the meaning of the slang term. This type of relationship is exactly what it sounds like. It is when two friends with no commitment engage in sexual activity.

There are a lot of teens that will say they don't want a commitment or a "label." They prefer a relationship where "no strings are attached." Casual relationships are more common than one might think especially among already sexually active teens. According to the Princeton Survey Research Associates International, approximately half of young teens (ages 13-16) who have had oral sex or sexual intercourse have been involved in a casual sexual relationship. These casual relationships typically involve oral sex (78%) and/or sexual intercourse (79%).

There are many reasons teens give as to why they engage in a "friends with benefits" relationship. For example, some want to avoid the complications of a serious relationship often because they think they are too young to get involved with someone in a committed way. Others are willing to get physically involved, but want to avoid getting emotionally involved. (We all know the problem with this is that it does not always work that way). Some are curious about this type of relationship and others want to make the relationship they have with their friend closer. However, probably the biggest reason for engaging in a causal relationship has to do with sexual urges. Teens often readily admit that they have strong sexual desires and want to fulfill them with someone they know and trust. Therefore, they find some friend who is willing to be their partner and meet their sexual needs. This all sounds very adult; doesn't it?

This brings me to the next emerging sexual trend among our youth, which is that both boys and girls are more forward and forceful. This forwardness combined with casualness leads to several types of sex and sex games that are in the mainstream among our youth today. Probably the most important type of sex to think about in this combination of forwardness and forcefulness is oral sex. Several experts have begun to talk about how 'oral sex is the next goodnight kiss.' In fact, there is even a book written about this phenomenon with our teens by Sharlene Azam who followed several subjects around in Canada for four years to learn more about this particular trend.

In recent years, we have seen an influx in news reports around the country suggesting that oral sex is something our youth is desensitized to. It is currently viewed as "in vogue" among school aged kids. One of the main reasons that this has become more mainstream and widespread is that teens do not consider oral sex to be sex. Many teens believe that if they engage in oral sex, it is o.k. because they are still virgins. In other words, they will say "it doesn't count." This is particularly important and true for our pre-teens who are still often at the age where they are not ready or willing to have sexual intercourse.

Today, an estimated 70% of teens, ages 13 to 16, know the definition of oral sex. For many teens (43%), oral sex is not seen as being as big a deal as sexual intercourse. Therefore, they engage in it more willingly. So why are teens choosing to have oral sex in a more casual way? There is a combination of reasons that seem to come up for most of our youth. These include, but are not limited to desire, love, curiosity, and pressure from their partner.

According to the Princeton Survey Research Associates International study mentioned earlier, an estimated 21% say they had oral sex for the first time because they wanted to be more popular or to be accepted. A much larger 76% said they did so because the other person wanted to. 64% said they were curious and 71% of teens said they did it because they met the right person. Other statistics reveal that 70% wanted to satisfy a sexual desire, 68% didn't want to have to worry about pregnancy, and 49% did so because they wanted to remain virgins. Lastly, 4 in 10 teens say they have had oral sex to avoid having sexual intercourse. Most 13 and 14 year olds who have had oral sex did so to avoid intercourse at least once. Boys and girls are equally likely to have opted for oral sex over intercourse.

One question that comes up among parents often is "do our teens understand the risks of oral sex?" The good news is that most teens *do* seem to be aware of the risks. However, instead of focusing on what they are at risk for, they tend to focus on what they are NOT at risk for if they engage in oral sex (i.e. pregnancy). It is true that a person cannot become pregnant from having oral sex. However, it does not stop our youth from getting STD's, which most of them do not consider. While most teens know about the risks, many do not take the proper precautions to pro-tect themselves. Nine in 10 (89%) teens who have had oral sex say they know STD's can be spread through oral sex. Yet only 3 in 10 (30%) always use protection when they have oral sex. To be honest, this last statistic seems high to me. In my professional experience in working with hundreds of kids over the course of almost two decades, I have NEVER had anyone confirm the use of protection when they have performed or received oral sex.   I ask about the use of protection regularly when working with teens so that I can take the time to educate them about STD's.   I know several of my colleagues do the same. Therefore, I decided to consult with the ones who regularly work with teens and they all concurred with my finding.   They also have NEVER had a teen admit to protecting themselves during oral sex.

Oral sex is *not* the only way that we are observing casual sex among our youth.   The combination of being more forward and casual with sex also leads to sex games becoming more advanced and provocative.   Remember the days of spin the bottle?   Well, those days are over in middle school and high school. You might still find this game in older elementary school, but it has been replaced in middle schools and high schools with games like "Happy Endings" and "The Rainbow Game."   "Happy Endings" is a game played where a group of boys typically invite over one or two girls to join them socially often at someone's house or at a party.   The boys form a circle around the girl(s).   The girl(s) willingly stands in the middle of the circle.   She then proceeds to go from boy to boy doing whatever physically and/or sexually she would like to do to them.   She has the freedom to do whatever she would like to do.   For example, she might give one boy a hug, another boy a kiss, and another boy a blow job.   All the boys in the circle are hoping for a "Happy Ending" hence the name.   The boys watch the girl(s) as she makes her way around the circle.   Nothing is private.   Often there is cheering and a commentary by one or more of the boys in the circle.

The rainbow game is another highly sexually provocative game. It is when girls go to the nearest drugstore to pick up different colored lipsticks preferably in the colors of the rainbow. They then proceed to apply one of the lipstick colors onto their lips and give oral sex to a boy or to multiple boys (usually on the same night). They then apply a different color and engage in more oral sex – sometimes to the same boy and sometimes to others. As a result, they are creating the colors of the rainbow on a boy(s) penis.

There is one more game I would like to mention. Although I am not sure we should call it a game. It is more of a nonverbal statement that girls make to boys about what they are willing to do sexually. Girls have adopted a fashionable way to make this statement by wearing different colored jelly bracelets around their wrists. This new social phenomenon involves "snapping" the bracelet off the wearer, enabling the snapper to earn a sexual favor from the snappee based on the color of the snapped off bracelet. Each color has a different coded meaning. I have made a list of some examples below.

* **Yellow** - indicates the wearer is willing to HUG
* **Pink** - indicates the wearer is willing to give a hickey
* **Orange** - indicates the wearer is willing to KISS
* **Purple** - indicates the wearer is willing to kiss a partner of either sex
* **Red** - indicates the wearer is willing to perform a LAP DANCE

* **Green** - indicates that ORAL SEX can be performed on a girl
* **Clear** - indicates a willingness to do "whatever the snapper wants"
* **Blue** - indicates ORAL SEX performed on a guy
* **Black** - indicates that the wearer will have regular "missionary" sex
* **White** - indicates the wearer will "FLASH" what they have
* **Glittery Yellow** - indicates HUGGING and KISSING is acceptable
* **Glittery Pink** - willing to "flash" (show) a body part
* **Glittery Purple** - wearer is willing to French (open mouth) kiss
* **Glittery Blue** - wearer is willing to perform anal sex
* **Glittery Green** - indicates that the wearer is willing to "69" (mutual oral sex)
* **Glittery Clear** - indicates that the wearer will let the snappee "feel up" or touch any body part they want

Most of the time, the games and the sexual acts that our teens are participating in are with full consent between the two participants. This is usually not something that a teen is being physically forced to do. However, this does not mean that there may not be some emotional pressure and covert coercion placed on one of the individuals involved. Most people tend to think that it would be the girl who is pressured. However, this is not always the case. Often it is the boy feeling pressured into engaging in some form of sexual activity. The issue of being pressured into doing something sexually that the person is uncomfortable with will be addressed in detail later in this book.

The next trend that I would like to talk about is probably the most alarming. In fact, it is criminal because it is moving our female youth toward prostitution. There are two parts to this trend. If the girls engage in the first part, then they are more likely to engage in the second. In this trend, the girls are very much aware of what they are doing. So what are they doing?

It is not uncommon for girls in our society to get money, clothing, and/or drugs for performing some sexual act. This usually starts off innocently enough in the girl's mind where a boy might say, "if you take off your shirt, I'll give you ten bucks." The girl thinks about it and decides that it is no different from wearing a bathing suit; after all she has a bra under her shirt. She wants the $10, sees no harm in it, and does as she is asked to receive the money.

Unfortunately, it usually does not stop there. The girl, who often has been drinking, is now asked to do other sexual things beyond a strip tease. This time she is offered $40 to give someone a blow job. This may seem like a huge leap from taking off her shirt, but if she got money for things in between, she builds a tolerance to it and enjoys the benefits of the money. In other words, the girl justifies her actions and believes that there is nothing wrong with what she is doing. She thinks about the new pair of jeans she wants, but cannot afford, and how long it will take her to save the money from her measly allowance and minimum wage paycheck. She goes for it convincing herself that it is not that big of a deal and that she won't do it again. The problem is that there will always be another pair of jeans that she wants and an "easy" way to make a lot of money in a very short period of time. Many of the girls who engage in this behavior are proud of what they are doing. In fact, they think they are "smart" and the boys are "stupid" for paying for something they would probably get for free later that night anyway.

The second part of this trend moves even further towards prostitution and actually becomes prostitution in its full force. There are girls in our society who are being recruited by other girls to enter prostitution rings. I know this sounds crazy, but it *is* happening. If a girl sees another girl giving a strip tease, lap dance, or blow job to a boy at a party for money, she might be approached by that girl and enlisted to make a lot more money by prostituting herself to others. She is assured that the men she will have sex with are not "dirty old men" off the streets, but higher class individuals who will treat them well (although this is not always the case).

Clearly this scenario is different because it means having sex with men she does not know. Therefore, once again she will be making a huge leap. She will go from making money at a party among classmates who she might "hook up" with anyway later that night for free to having sex with random men for hundreds of dollars. The girl usually is more inclined to make this leap if she is really in need of money. For example, if she has a drug habit or recently crashed her parent's car and wants to get it fixed before they get home from their trip, then she might fall into the trap. Again, in this scenario she is a very willing

participant. She is making the choice to engage in prostitution. I stress this point because there are some girls who
are being recruited by other girls and they do not have a
clue of what they are getting themselves into. Perhaps this
part of the trend (toward prostitution) is even more
upsetting to learn about.

Whenever I give trainings to parents or mental health
workers on this topic, this is the point in which they all
say, "you mean there is something even more upsetting
than all of this?" The answer unfortunately is "yes." In
this next circumstance, girls are still being recruited by
other girls, however, this time the girl being recruited has
no idea that she is being recruited, and therefore, is not
receiving any money. Instead, it is the recruiter who is
making all the money and using the other girl as her pawn
to get it. The girl who is being recruited actually has no
idea that money is even being exchanged. In other words,
the girl is completely unaware that she is being victimized
in a sex scheme. Let me explain how this scheme works.

Usually an older girl (i.e. a high schooler) finds a
younger girl (i.e. a middle schooler) and strikes up a conversation with her. This might happen at a 7'11 or a local
park. The older girl tells the younger girl that she seems
incredibly mature for her age, which of course every
middle schooler loves to hear from a high schooler. She
also tells her how much older she looks than other girls
her own age (again something every middle schooler loves
to hear). The older girl then proceeds to befriend the
younger girl and invites her to a high school party. She
makes sure that the girl knows how special this invitation

is because "never in a million years would a middle schooler be invited to a high school party." However, since she is not the "typical" middle schooler (meaning she is mature, older looking, usually very attractive) she is invited to come. She is even permitted to bring a friend if she wants to as long as her friend is as "mature" and as "chill as she is.

The high schooler puts a lot of pressure on the middle schooler to not embarrass her at this party. She tells her that there will be older, more mature, "hot" guys at the party she will introduce her to if she is interested. She then informs the girl that there is one boy in particular that she thinks will like her a lot. She tells her that she will point him out at the party and then introduce them to each other. She explains that "he doesn't like just anybody" and prepares her not to be "too disappointed" if it does not work out. She guides the girl on what to wear to the party (usually something skimpy and promiscuous). She guides her on how to act and what to say. Of course the middle schooler wants to go to the party and meet this high school boy. Therefore, she accepts the invitation.

Inevitably, the middle school girl sneaks out of her house the night of the party because there is "no way" she is going to miss the opportunity to hang out with "hot high school guys." When she gets there she is greeted by her new high school friend who keeps her promise and after feeding her several drinks to get her drunk, introduces her to the hot guy she told her about. This "hot guy" has been waiting for her to come to the party that night. The female high school friend told this boy that she would get a younger, more impressionable girl to the party and then he could see if the girl would be interested in "hooking up" with him.

The stage has been set for high success, but now it is up to the guy to "work his magic." The guy approaches the younger girl and makes his move. The unsuspecting girl simply believes this boy is interested in her for all the reasons that her new friend told her he would be; she is "mature, chill, and fun to be around." The story usually ends with the two individuals "hooking up." This sexual "hook up" could be anything from 'making out' to having sex. If the guy gets oral sex from the girl or has sexual intercourse with her, then he has to pay the female high school friend that brought her to the party.

Recruiters receive payment in many forms. They may receive money, clothing, jewelry, alcohol or drugs. The scariest part of this new emerging trend (I know it is all scary) is that the whole thing is oddly consensual. Nobody is forcing anyone else to do something that they do not want to do. Yes, it is being done under false pretenses, but nonetheless the girls are very willing participants. In fact, many of them will call these guys over and over again after the initial "hook up" in hopes to see them again. The boys often have no problem with this and do indeed see the girls again. Unfortunately, it is often just for sexual reasons and not to develop a healthy committed relationship. In this example, I talk about high school girls recruiting middle school girls. It is important to note that this also occurs between college students and high school students. In addition, although it is much more common for older girls to recruit younger girls, there are also times where girls are the same age. In any case, most of us would never beleive we would be hearing that girls are recruiting other girls into sexual activity. We are much more used to hearing about boys seducing girls to be with them sexually, not girls seducing other girls to be with boys sexually, which in essence is exactly what is happening. It is a highly unfortunate state of affairs when this occurs and one that we will hopefully be able to prevent in our future with education, insight, and knowledge.

Many people wonder what factors play a role in the emerging sexual trends among our youth. Although this is the main focus of our next chapter, I would like to give one example here that directly connects to the remaining trends we will focus on in this chapter. The factor that I would like to spend some time talking about is the role of technology. I believe that technology plays a very large part in our society's new sexual movement. Technological advances in our society have been viewed by most as very positive throughout the past many years. However, these advances have had its downfalls. In connection to teen sexuality, it provides a certain level of anonymity and protection. This anonymity and protection leads to higher levels of forwardness and disrespect, which seems to be yet another emerging sexual trend among our youth.

Think about how many of our teens use text messaging on their cell phones as well as online communication through websites such a Facebook and MySpace. Kids are not communicating face to face like they used to which gives them the courage to say things to each other that they might not say in person. Most teens agree that this type of technology reduces their inhibitions and as a result allows them to say things that they never would have dreamed of to someone else. The content of what teens might say, may or may not be sexual. In addition, it may be positive or negative. In either case, teens do not have to worry about the other person's reaction, which is why their inhibitions are lowered. If an interchange happens in person that is viewed as offensive or disrespectful, then the person might experience consequences such as a slap in the face. Knowing that this is a possibility with a face to face interaction, but not with an online interaction or texting interchange, the teen almost always opts for the latter.

Many text messages are of a sexual content. When this occurs, it is called sex messaging. We will discuss sex messaging in more detail later in this chapter. However, for now I will say sex messaging often contains offensive and highly disrespectful comments. This is particularly true when boys are sex messaging girls. The high level of disrespect in communication among our youth is another trend that we are seeing in our society.

As boys make more casual sexual advances to girls, they often do it in a way that is crude and forceful. Interestingly, when asked if they think they are being crude and forceful most boys would answer 'no.' They do not see it this way. They would more likely see their advances as "funny" and/or "cool." It is not uncommon for boys to start conversations with girls by saying "wanna suck me?" and ending conversations with "wanna fuck?" In my experience, the girls that report this happening most frequently seem to be middle schoolers (particularly 8th graders). However, it happens among younger and older grades as well.

It might surprise you to know that it is *not* only our teenage boys who view this type of questioning as "funny." Many of our teenage girls also view it as "funny," and therefore do not seem to mind when it happens to them. Many of these girls report that they see it as a compliment. They say "it is the way I know for sure that a boy is interested in me." Unfortunately, as adults we know that they are not asking themselves "interested in what part of me?"

Other girls care more that boys are making disrespectful comments and advances. However, most of these girls react indifferently to it. Not because it doesn't bother them, but because it is something they have become used to. For example, when asked if this bothers them, most are quick to say "what do you expect, they're boys." Isn't it interesting that they are more apt to say this (excusing the boys behavior) rather than answering the question. Unfortunately, this "boys will be boys" attitude only perpetuates the problem because it does not hold the boy responsible and it allows this type of communication to continue. We have to ask ourselves as a society, is it more upsetting to see an increase in disrespectful communication or a laissez-faire attitude that goes along with it?

As pre-teen and teenage boys are becoming increasingly disrespectful, we are seeing our pre-teen and teenage girls becoming more assertive. Clearly assertiveness is not a bad thing. Wouldn't it be great if our girls asserted themselves when boys were acting in a disrespectful way all the time? Sometimes this happens, sometimes it does not as we saw in my last example. It is our job as the adults in our society to help our girls understand that it is 'o.k.' to stand up for themselves and stand against this type of communication. I think it is wonderful that girls are able to voice their opinions more now than they ever were in the past. Our society has made a huge shift in teaching girls to go get what they want. We teach them to get a career, to go to college, make money, and be successful in society. Teaching them to go out and get what they want applies to relationships and sex as well. Girls are using sex to gain power and control in their relationships. Girls are using sex to gain money, clothes, jewelry, but they do NOT see this as prostitution as discussed earlier.

Another emerging sexual trend among our youth is sexting and sex messaging. We have already talked a little bit about sex messaging. Sex messaging is highly common among our teens. It is also common among adults in our society. Parents need to recognize that their children are often following their example. Most teens are very well aware that their parents send sex messages back and forth to one another. I often hear stories about the sex messages that teens have seen sent between their parents or between one parent and a mistress. You may think your children have no idea as to what you are communicating with someone else, but they do. They check your cell phones and look at your text messages. Parents are not the only ones who snoop.   In fact, kids are very good at it because they are so curious.

Let's take a moment to understand why this trend toward sex messaging has developed. Before cell phones and text messages, kids would pass notes back and forth in class. Sometimes there would be some sexual content in those notes. However, it seemed to be much more innocent. For example, a typical note might ask the question, "who do you like in math class?" Underneath the question would be a list of names to choose from. The receiver would circle one of the names and then pass the note back to the sender.   Note passing has turned into sex messaging (also called flirtexting) which has much more sexually charged material in it.   For example, instead of asking who you think is cute or who you like, people will ask who they would have sex with. In addition, this type of messaging happens with much greater frequency due to two reasons. Note taking took time, energy, and a certain sense of sneakiness due to not wanting to get caught by the teacher. This is not the case with sex messaging. Nothing is being passed from one person to the other. Instead, it all goes through the wonderful world of cyberspace. At most, the teacher will catch the student with their cell phone out in class and confiscate it for the rest of the period.

U.S. teens (ages 13 to 17) had the highest levels of text messaging in Q2 2008, sending and receiving an average of 1,742 text messages per month. In comparison, teens took part in an average of 231 mobile phone calls per month, during the same time period. What does this say about our society? We are definitely becoming a disen-franchised society with much less personal contact. (See chapter 3 for more of a discussion on this).

Sex messaging is very different from sexting. Sexting is when an individual sends sexually charged material such as nude pictures and videos via cell phone text messages or postings online.   This sexually charged material can be solicited by others and/or offered consensually. In either case, there may be a reason that the person is sexting. One of the reasons may be that they are looking for attention. This may end up being positive or negative attention, which may or may not matter to the individual. However, they are trying to gain some interest from someone else through sexting.

Kids often see stuff on MySpace and other places online where other kids are posing sexually in photos often in the nude, strip teasing, or performing real or mock sex. Many of these kids see this as their 15 megabytes of fame. They think it's cool to be famous and know that it is not out of the norm. What teens do not realize is that there are both psychological and legal ramifications to sexting. Psychologically, the person may experience feel-ings of embarrassment, humiliation, shame, and guilt which can all lead to Depression and/or Anxiety. This is not usually something the teen thinks about ahead of time. Initially they do not see it as a big deal. However, they do not always realize how many people may have access to the photo or video they sent out and in turn, what the reaction of others will be toward them.

Take Mary for example. She attends a local public high school. She decided to send a boy she liked a nude video of herself. She had no idea that he would send it to several of his friends who each sent it to several of their friends and so on until it reached over 300 people at her school. She was completely harassed on campus every day by both boys and girls. They emotionally abused her by calling her names such as "slut" and "whore." They physically abused her by throwing objects at her in the hallway, pushing her into lockers, and hitting and kicking her when she walked by. In addition, she was threatened by certain girls when she talked to certain guys. They accused her of trying to have sex with their boyfriends. She was sexually abused on numerous occasions by other boys at her school. She was grabbed, groped, and fondled while being told, "Sluts like you want it."

Mary began to develop tremendous anxiety and depression. She had thoughts of suicide and was hospitalized. Following her hospitalization, she transferred schools. Unfortunately, people at her new school heard about the video she had made and some of the harassment continued there. Her parents decided to move out of the state to help her start a new life. Mary was lucky. Her parents had the ability to pick up and start new. However, this is not always the case.

The biggest fear for most parents is that sexting can lead to suicide. There was a famous case about a girl who did complete a suicide due to a sexting incident she was involved in. Her name was Jesse Logan. She attended Cincinnati High School and committed suicide in July of

2008. She was harassed in a similar way to Mary. She became so depressed that she decided to speak out. She went on television to share her story. However, the depression was too great for her and she took her life not too long after the broadcast. Last fall, the National Campaign to Prevent Teen and Unplanned Pregnancy surveyed teens and young adults about sexting. The results revealed that (1) 39 % of teens are sending or posting sexually suggestive photos, (2) 48 % report receiving such photos, and (3) 15 % admit to forwarding these photos (usually after a break up).

There are several legal Ramifications due to sexting that most parents and teens are fully *un*aware of. Creating a nude photo or video of oneself or of someone else if they are under the age of 18 is production of child pornography. Sending that nude photo or video to someone else is distribution of child pornography. Receiving and holding onto that nude photo or video is possession of child pornography. Let's go back to the example of Mary. Mary produced child pornography when she made the video of herself. This is 100% against the law. She then distributed child pornographic material when she sent it to the boy she liked. This is also 100% against the law. The boy and all of his friends who sent it to their friends not only distributed child pornographic material once, but 4 or 5 times (one count per each time sent). The people who received the video (all 300 students at the school) were in possession of child pornographic material which is also 100% against the law.

Clearly most teens are unaware that they are breaking the law. However, this does not stop prosecutors from charging them. It may stop a prosecutor from sentencing them to several years in juvenile hall or jail according to the circumstances, but it is illegal and therefore, punishable by law. Let's look at the famous case of Genarlow Wilson in Georgia. Genarlow was convicted of having consensual oral sex with a 15-year-old girl when he was 17. He videotaped his encounter with the girl at a party. Genarlow was sentenced to 10 years in prison and required to register as a sex offender. He was released after serving two years following an appeal to the state supreme court.

There are no known cases involving federal charges against a minor for child pornography. Most of the recent cases were brought under state laws by local prosecutors, usually in juvenile court. Since juvenile cases are not part of the public record, it's not known what kinds of sentences have resulted from such cases, but generally juveniles who commit crimes get convicted of delinquency, not the actual crime they commit. Although this is good news for our minors, especially the ones who are unaware that they may be breaking the law; I think this may change. With greater education and awareness comes greater penalty. That is why it is vitally important that we educate our teens about sexting and the legal ramifications around this.

Most teens seem to accept that production and distribution of nude photos or videos is illegal. They seem to have a harder time accepting that if they receive a photo or video they can get in trouble for posession. I use the analogy to marijuana with them when this comes up. I tell them if someone gives them pot, they are in possession of an illegal substance whether it is theirs or not. If it is in their possession, it is their responsibility. I also reiterate that people who take or share nude self-portraits when they're minors could be prosecuted as adults and face harsher penalties if they're still in possession of the images when they reach the age of 18.

Having to register as a sex offender alters a person's life forever. There is a public record (meaning anyone and everyone has access to it) indicating that this person has committed a sex crime against a minor. Due to the public record, the person frequently is harassed by neighbors, often finds it difficult to get a job, and loses many relation-ships due to the offense. Teens simply do not understand that this may be a consequence of their actions when sexting.

Another thing that teens do not fully understand that can lead to a variety of negative consequences is when they mix alcohol with sex. According to several research centers nationwide, teens reported at least half their friends are sexually active in high school. The National Center for alcohol abuse wanted to understand how alcohol coincided with sex. They reported in 2006 that 66% of teens who were sexually active tried alcohol and 31% of sexually active teens got drunk at least once in the month prior to their interview. In addition, teens reported that they engaged in more sexual activity than they may have if they were sober. Now thats what I call a sobering statistic!

According to the Department of Justice, approximately 1 in 3 girls will experience some sort of sexual assault before the age of 18. This includes forcible sex as well as non-consensual touching. These statistics are certainly striking to most. However, perhaps what is even more striking is the fact that only an estimated 20% of victims file a crime report leaving us to wonder how many more females are being victimized than our statistics illustrate.

Girls are not the only victims. Boys may experience rape as well and are even less likely to report this crime. There are a variety of reasons why rape victims choose not to report such as fear, avoidance, guilt, and self-blame. Sometimes the person does not even realize they were sexually assaulted. This is often the case when she/he was intoxicated, their perpetrator was intoxicated or they were both intoxicated. It is estimated that 80 - 90% of sexual assaults are by an acquaintance and approximately 75% of all sexual assaults have some form of alcohol involved. In preparation for our teens moving on to college, I have listed some alarming facts that parents can share with their children in an attempt to keep them safe and unharmed. You can find this list at the end of the book (Appendix A).

In addition to teens reporting that alcohol may influence their thoughts and feelings about sex, they indicate that pornography also plays a role. This indication brings us to yet another emerging sexual trend among our youth. The viewing of pornographic material is on the rise. I am not talking about child pornographic material being produced, distributed, and possessed by many of our unknowing teens such as in the sexting example we earlier discussed. In this category, I am talking about adult pornographic material, which many of our teens are becoming addicted to especially our teenage boys.

One of the reasons that I think we have seen such an increase in pornography is that it is highly accessible. In part we have technology to thank for this. Once again, I will take you back to the olden days when a boy had to find a way to get his hands on a playboy magazine at the corner store in the adult section. This was not easy to do. Therefore, it was usually one boy who accessed these magazines either by swiping them off the racks or by sneaking them out of an older brother's room or dad's secret hiding place in the garage. Even this took some strategy and know how.

Today, kids don't have to go through that much trouble. They simply turn on their computer and search "sex" or "pornography" and magically it appears for them right in front of their eyes. Below are some statistics on pornography. This emerging sexual trend is not only on the rise with our youth, but with adults in our society as well. Therefore, I have also included some statistics on the amount of pornography adults are viewing in our society today. These statistics are important as you will see later in this book when we talk about the need for parents to be good role models for their kids (chater 4 and 5). It might surprise you to know that both males and females are viewing pornographic material more often due to its accessibility and it being less of a taboo in our country.

CHILDREN INTERNET PORNOGRAPHY STATISTICS

* Average age of first internet exposure to pornography is 11 years old.
* Largest consumer of internet porn is 35-49 year olds.
* 80% of 15-17 year olds have had multiple hard-core exposures
* 90% (most while doing their homework) of 8-16 year olds have viewed pornography online
* 29% of 7-17 year olds freely give out their home address.
* 14% of 7-17 year olds freely give out their e-mail address.
* There are approximately 26 (including Pokemon and Action Man) children's character names linked to thousands of pornography sites.

ADULT PORNOGRAPHY STATISTICS

* 40 million US adults regularly visit internet pornography websites
* 72% are male, 28% are female
* 20% of men and 13% of women admit to accessing pornography at work
* 17% of US adults readily admit to pornography addiction.

When collecting the statistics listed above, I became interested in who produces pornography in our country and whether or not this plays a role in this emerging trend. What I found was interesting, but not surprising. Below is a list of the top video pornography producers in the world. Notice which country is in the lead. Being number one in this category is certainly not going to win us any medals, but it does help us to understand why there is a rampant change in our society with a huge focus and acceptance on viewing pornographic material.

TOP VIDEO PORNOGRAPH PRODUCERS

1. United States: Vivid Entertainment, Hustler, Playboy, Wicked Pictures, Red Light District
2. Brazil
3. The Netherlands
4. Spain
5. Japan
6. Russia
7. Germany
8. United Kingdom
9. Canada
10. Australia

I talk to teenagers a lot about pornography and their experience with it. Most of the teens that I have spoken with both personally and professionally admit that they have seen pornographic material at some point in their lives. Interestingly what many of them comment on is not what they see, but how they perceive it. Both boys and girls agree that pornography leads to misconceptions about sex and body image. In regards to sex, they state that it confuses boys about what girls want and how easily they may be willing to engage in sexual behavior. For example, one of my male patients came in to talk with me about something he found to be highly embarrassing. He was asked by a girl to come over to her house and watch a movie. When he got there, he found out that the girls parents were not home. They sat on the couch in the girl's family room and started the feature length film. About five minutes into the movie, the girl stood up and told the boy that she would be right back. She left the room and the boy's heart started to pound. She returned a few minutes later to find the boy lying naked on her couch. She was horrified and screamed "what the hell are you doing?" The boy jumped up and covered himself with his clothes. He said "I thought you were going to get into something more comfortable." These were not words he came up with on his own. He had heard them before in several of the pornographic movies his dad had lying around the house.

My patient had seen a lot of pornography. He was 16 years old and viewed pornography for the first time when he was 11 years old. He had no idea what this girl wanted or desired. He just knew what he saw in the videos. From his perspective, he was invited over to her home with no parents around and she left the room where they were "just beginning to get close." Her reason for leaving the room was simply to make some popcorn for them to snack on. She had no intention of doing anything sexual with him that required their clothes off. This confused the boy because this is not what he learned from the multiple videos he had viewed in his lifetime. In addition, nobody had ever talked to him about sex before. In fact, the only thing he did know about sex was what he was taught in health class, which as we all know, mostly focuses on anatomy, the reproductive system, and the physical process of sex. He admitted that pornography strongly influenced the way he thought about sex in general and thus how he acted in this specific situation.

Most teens seem to agree that pornography influences the way they think about sex. Another way that it influences their thought process is in regards to body image. Both boys and girls admit that they are misled as to what the average body looks like when naked. This is due to the fact that the photos and videos in the pornographic material that they view portray actors and models and not the average person. In addition, when the pornographic material is in a photo, the photos are often photoshopped to make the person look "better" than they actually are and when the pornographic material is in a video, body doubles are often used for the same purpose. This type of misconception often leads to embarrassment, disappointment, and concern for the teenager. Both boys and girls often worry that they or the other person they are with will not be seen as "good enough." They worry that they will not meet the expectations or desires of their partner. They compare their bodies to the bodies of porn stars and in turn, feel badly about themselves. Unfortuntely, these "bad" feelings do not stop our teens from viewing pornography. In fact, it seems to be the opposite. Pornography is being viewed more by our youth now than ever before regardless of the misconceptions and negative influences it may have on them.

One of the most concerning factors regarding the rise of pornographic material being viewed by our youth, is the fact that there has also been a rise in their addiction to it. Pornography addiction is a serious matter. It is not something that a person can easily recover from without proper treatment. If you are concerned that your teen is addicted to pornography ask him/her the following questions.

1. Do you feel compulsively drawn to look at pornography?
2. Does the behavior consume your thoughts or interfere with your ability to function normally (i.e., keep you from doing your homework, chores, spend time with family or friends, etc.)?
3. Realistically, could you stop the behavior today if you wanted to?

If the answer to the first two questions is yes and the answer to the third question is no, then your child may be addicted to pornography. In this case, it is important to seek a counselor that specializes with addiction for your child. If the answer to the third question is yes, ask your child to put his/her answer to a test. Tell him/her to refrain from looking at any type of pornographic material for one month. Explain to your child that he/she is not in trouble, but that you would like him/her to find out for themselves their level of dependence on pornography. Be sure to reiterate that this test is not for you or anybody else. It is for the sake of your child so that he/she can identify if there is a problem.

If your child can easily refrain from viewing pornography for an entire month where questions one and two are not an issue, then they probably are NOT addicted. Note how I said that refraining from the behavior is not the *only* thing that indicates the lack of a problem. Most people can do anything for one month. The key is that your child can refrain from the behavior for one month while not being drawn to it or consumed with thoughts about it.

If your child struggles with refraining from the behavior for a period of one month or less, then they may be able to identify for themselves that there is a problem. Often kids do not realize that they are addicted to something because they assume that they can stop at any time. It is often not until they put themselves to this test that they truly can see if they are addicted or not.

3

WHY ARE WE SEEING EMERGING SEXUAL TRENDS AMONG OUR YOUTH?

We have talked about the emerging sexual trends among our youth in great detail in the last chapter.

I recognize that this is not pleasurable reading material for any adult in our society who cares about our youth and has their best interest in mind. However, it is important to identify these trends so that we can better understand why they are occurring. In this chapter of the book, we will investigate the reasons behind these changes. Let's start with the first one.

We currently live in a society that focuses on seeking immediate gratification. This means that we are currently raising our children to be highly impatient individuals. To deal with our growing impatience, our culture has increasingly emphasized a "quick fix" to even the smallest problem. Therefore, our children are not learning how to deal with their own distress. In turn, they have very low tolerance for frustration. Let's look some basic examples of this starting with a simple family dinner.

For most of us, taking the time to prepare a home cooked meal often does not occur when we are busy, harassed, and quite honestly, hungry.   This is why we are becoming a nation of fast food meals. Fast food restaurants provide us with a quick fix solution. It is very easy to go to the drive through window at McDonalds or Jack in the box and feed your whole family in less than 10 minutes. Most of the time, we don't even wait until we get home to start our dinner. A french fry or even a burger is in our mouth before our car reaches our home. I am certain that if the adult driving the car was questioned about the reason for beginning dinner on the drive home instead of waiting until the whole family was sitting together around the dinner table, they would say that they were hungry, hit all the red lights, and half the family was off doing other things so they wouldn't be eating together anyway. Doesn't this further illustrate the point?

We as a society are becoming increasingly impatient because we seek immediate gratification. Let's look at another example. How many of us have sat at those endless red lights and felt like we could barely stand to even hit one more on the way home especially if there was a screaming infant in the backseat of our car. If this example doesn't fit for you, then consider this next one. Television commercials have become too long for us. A great inventor in our society not too long ago developed something called 'TiVo' and 'My DVR?' Clearly this person was very aware of what the people in our county have been wanting for years; a way to fast forward through commercials. Now individuals can watch a whole program and several others (sometimes at the same time) in a shortened period of time. Does anyone watch live TV anymore? According to our teens, not many of them do.

Also according to our teens, any feeling that is uncomfortable for them, they attend to immediately through some form of action or behavior. This immediate attention offers them immediate relief. This is true for adults in our society as well. Remember it is the adults that are modeling these types of behaviors for our youth. Think about the anxious or depressed individual who quickly reaches for an over the counter pill, an alcoholic drink or a bag of chips and let's not forget about seeking out sex. All of these things are used by individuals in our society to feel "good."

Unfortunately, many individuals including our youth view this type of "quick fix" or immediate gratification as a positive and healthy thing. I suppose in some cases it can be. After all who wants to experience back pain when it can disappear shortly after taking two Motrin. However, it is not always that simple or beneficial. For example, what if the Motrin does not work fast enough or is not strong enough to take away *all* the pain. In this case, the person might go to their doctor and ask for a stronger pain medicine to achieve their "quick fix." In turn, this "quick fix" may become an addiction because they start to pop the pills like candy in an attempt to avoid *all* pain. This attempt to avoid distress is actually what causes a lowered frustration tolerance. This is just one example of how this happens; Let's look at another one.

I remember years ago being asked to come in to provide conflict resolution to a group of parents. These parents had their children on the same pee-wee soccer team. Therefore, their children were all around 5 and 6 years old. The season ended and the parents had to decide if they were going to give their kids trophies. The team was in last place because it had lost every game. Half the parents wanted to give the children on the team trophies and the other half of the parents did not.

The half that advocated for trophies made a very compelling argument. They stated that the kids tried really hard all season long and that they deserved to be rewarded for their efforts. The other half of the parents who did not want to award trophies also made a compelling argument. They stated that although the kids did try hard, they lost. In fact, not only did they lose, they came in very last place because they didn't win a single game. These parents strongly believed that when a person loses, they should not be rewarded with a prize because this is not indicative of what happens in real life.

It is one of life's hardest lessons to learn how to lose gracefully and these parents wanted to teach their children this lesson early in life. They felt very strongly about *not* rewarding their child for coming in last place. The first set of parents agreed that it is an important life lesson to learn how to lose gracefully, but they did not think pee wee soccer (at the age of 5) was the necessary time and place to learn this lesson. Instead, they wanted to come from a place of love and caring for their young children. In other words, they did not want their kids to feel bad. They knew that if their child did not receive a trophy, and their child's friends on the opposing teams did, that they would be highly upset and disappointed. Therefore, to avoid this type of feeling, they wanted to give them a trophy.

I think most people would agree that parents intuitively want their children to feel good. No parent wants to see their child upset and hurting. However, this is part of life. So what is the right answer? You will have to decide this for yourself. I can understand both sides of the argument and shared my views about them with the parents during the conflict resolution session. The session was initiated by the parents after they became physically aggressive with one another in their last meeting when trying to come to a solution on their own.

Finding a resolution to the problem did not take very long. The parents eventually agreed to disagree and each individual family made a personal choice as to whether or not they would give their child a trophy. I did take the time, however, with these parents to discuss something other than the conflict resolution. I took the time to talk to them about how we as parents tend to "rescue" our children from their own distress. I noted that although well intentioned, this is not always the best thing to do for our youth. Our kids need to learn how to deal with their own distress. If we continue to provide a "quick fix" solution for them, then they will follow our lead later in life and seek out immediate gratification every time they encounter feelings of anger, frustration, stress or sadness. As we have already learned, this lowers our frustration tolerance and before long our kids will not feel like they have the ability to deal with any distressing emotion.

Specifically in regards to the children on the pee wee soccer team, I talked with the parents about how they could best support their child through their feelings of hurt and disappointment. I explained to all of the parents that if a child is upset or frustrated, it is important for them to talk to them about their distress and teach them how to cope with the hurt they are experiencing. I recommend giving kids specific examples of times when you as an adult have been disappointed. Explian to them how you felt and what you did to get through it. This is not something that all children automatically know how to do. They need adults to model this for them and help them do the right thing.

If kids do not learn healthy and positive coping mechanisms early in life, they are more apt to seek out unhealthy and negative ones later in life. For example, for a "quick fix" they may turn to drugs to numb their pain, self-injure to physically express their emotional pain, and/or restrict their food to gain some sort of control over their life. (For more information on Self-Injury and Eating Disorders please reference the books *What Every Parent Needs to*

Know About Self Injurious Behavior and *What Every Parent Needs to Know About Eating Disorders,* Fastpencil.com).

The second possible cause for the emerging sexual trends in our society is the fact that our society is becoming increasingly disenfranchised. Extended family members are less available to our youth. The collapse of the extended family and the increasing isolation of the individual has given people, especially children, fewer confidants in times of difficulty. Let's go back to the example listed above regarding the decreased likelihood of having family dinners in our society today.

In the past, family dinners seemed to be held as a sacred event. It was important to families to have everyone gathered around the same table at the same time to share a meal. It was the one time that family members could talk about their day and experience true feelings of togetherness. Unfortunately, for many families, this ritual does not seem to exist anymore. Someone in the family is inevitably working late, at a sports practice or at a music lesson. This type of fragmented family leads to kids not having many people they can talk to anymore. Conversations about all things in their life are important; however, since this book is about emerging sexual trends among our youth, I will mainly focus on the fact that they do not have anyone to talk to about sex and relationships.

The modern teen may grow up relying very little on words, verbal expression, and the conventional exploration of their thoughts and feelings. Instead, the teen may depend more on *doing* rather than *saying*. Sex is one way of *doing* rather than *saying*. For example, one teen may say to another teen, "I will *show* you how much I care about you by giving you a blow job" or "If you really loved me, you would have sex with me."

The third possible cause for emerging sexual trends among our youth in society is that we have become a nation of addicts and "a-holics." Have you noticed that it has become "in" to be considered dysfunctional? In fact, it has become so "in" that individuals volunteer to share their dysfunction with millions of viewers on national television. Think about how many individuals volunteer to share their dysfunctional lives on the *Dr. Phil show* and how many individuals are willing to share their sex addiction with the entire nation by going on the *Dr. Drew show*.

Teen boys think it's cool to be a "player." Teen girls think it's cool to be sexy. Both boys and girls like the attention they get from one another in a sexual way. They have no problem "hooking up" with each other and then telling everyone about the sexual encounter they just had. In fact, many brag about it to all their friends. There is of course a minority of teens who prefer not "kissing and telling." However, if and when it comes out what they have done sexually with someone else, it is not viewed as negative as it would have been in the past.

Most teens understand that there are "no true secrets" these days among them. Although this is sad because it brings up an issue of the lack of trust our peers have for one another, it is commonplace and the "norm" for kids to share personal information with each other that was once held as private and/or sacred. We may have technology in part to thank for this once again. When one person finds something out, it is almost immediately posted online for all to know. In the past, things might blow over with time. However, with the invention of cyberspace, information is easy to access and therefore, teens find out each other's business in a matter of seconds. For example, it takes less than two minutes to share with hundreds of teens online what would have taken hours on the telephone in years past.

As we understand more about the reasons for the emerging sexual trends among our youth, we need to explore what sex gives to our kids. Sex gives many different things to all individuals in our society including our youth. One of the biggest things that it provides to our teens is tension release. It is no big surprise that sex feels good. Our society is changing. It is harder to be a kid. There is more tension, pressure, and distress in their lives from all sources including school, family, friends, sports, etc. Our teens are looking for ways to reduce this tension, pressure and distress. They find different outlets, some which are positive such as sports, music, and art, and some that are negative such as self-mutilation, eating problems, substance abuse, and yes....SEX. Sex is more accessible now than it ever has been before due to the trends we have listed above. We don't want our kids to become addicted to sex. Therefore, education around sex is important. We will discuss how to educate and talk to our children later in this book (see chapter 3 and 4).

Another thing that sex gives to individuals including our youth is a sense of connectedness. Sex allows us to feel close, connected, cared for, needed, and loved by another person. This is especially important for teenagers. In fact, it is exactly what our teens strive for during this developmental phase of their lives. Teenagers want to belong. They want to be accepted. They feel this way when they are loved and cared for by one of their friends or by a boyfriend/girlfriend. If sex helps them feel this way, they are more likely to engage in it. We all know that sex helps people to feel this way the majority of the time. Therefore, we need to prepare for the fact that it will be sought out by our teens more frequently if our society continues to move toward the beleif system that sex is "no big deal."

One last thing that sex gives to our youth is important to note because it is less common, but still cited often by our youth. Sex gives our teens something to do. In other words, it is a cure for boredom. This may surprise you to hear, but it is true. Many teens report to me that they engage in sexual activity because they are bored and there is nothing better to do in their town. Teens are looking for excitement. We have created a society that focuses on highly stimulating things. This increased stimulation in all aspects of life leads to more boredom among our youth.

Everything seems to be more stimulating for our youth these days. Athletic sports are a prime example of this. Recent studies illustrate that kids are leaning more toward the sports that are constantly moving, like soccer and bas-ketball versus baseball and ballet. My husband recently attended a coach's clinic for T-Ball and Single A ball. The trainer stressed one main point over and over again during the 8 hour workshop. He re-iterated to the coaches the importance of keeping the kids moving on the field. He said if the kids are not having fun, they will quickly become bored and drop out of the sport.

Baseball has had the highest drop out rate of any sport in the past decade and it is rich in American tradition. "Baseball is as American as apple pie" yet many of our kids are bored with it and have stopped viewing it as an American pastime. My kids play baseball currently and it is not uncommon for me to hear a kid standing in the outfield say "this is boring" or "how much longer till the game is over?" Baseball is not as exciting and fast paced as other sports are for them.

Movies have shifted in this way as well. Has anyone noticed how bored our 5-7 year olds have become watching the old Disney movies? Although adorable and classic, these movies do not have fast paced, exciting chase scenes in them. Today with improved special effects, we can now watch a movie and actually feel as if we are in the middle of the scene. Due to this fact, old movies often cause boredom among our youth and the classics are truly becoming a thing of the past. One might argue that this is more important for boys than girls, but in either case, I have personally witnessed a lack of attentiveness in both genders when they are viewing these films. Our kids seem to want something more stimulating. Once they have seen one stimulating movie, they become accustomed to them. Then the rest seem to be boring and unappealing. For example, recently my 7 year old son wanted to watch a movie in the theater with his friends. When we got to the theater one of his friends said "what? No 3-D. Oh come on!"

This boredom theory seems to be true for television shows as well. Maybe this is why *Tom and Jerry* seems to be one of the few cartoons our kids get excited to watch in their older childhood years. As our kids get older, we continue to see this problem. For example, let's look at the change in how movies and television shows are rated. What is now rated PG 13 would have been rated R when we were kids. This is not only due to the sexual content in the movie, but due to the violence and adult language in the show.

Several experts claim that high stimulation leads to over stimulation and that over stimulation leads to over-scheduling. Kids have little down time between the increase in their school work and homework load, their sports schedules, and their music and art lessons. This lack of down time is not healthy; however, it is what most kids have become accustomed to. When kids are not busy, they become bored. I think we can all agree that with boredom, trouble can follow. Although for centuries parents have said that a bored child can lead to some very unhealthy and unproductive behaviors, this is particularly true now in our changing society. Maybe this is why parents keep their children so busy in the first place because they are trying to avoid negativity in their leisure lives.

Keeping a child busy can have both positive and negative effects. The positive is to keep them out of trouble, but the negative is that it teaches them impatience. Just as our kids are *not* being taught how to deal with distressing emotion, they are *not* being taught how to deal with boredom. Our kids do not know how to feel bored and how to appreciate down time. In fact, many of them feel uneasy and even guilty when they are resting and relaxing. This in part may be due to what is being modeled for them. For example, if the important role models in their lives view relaxation as laziness, then they will adopt this belief system for themselves.

There is no doubt that most of us have very busy lifestyles. This has changed over the years and is true for more families now than ever before. However, in our busy lives, it is important to learn how to unwind. If we as adults can do this, then we can teach our children how to do this. Don't we all want our children to appreciate and capture moments of rest and relaxation? Unfortunately, they do not seem to come around as much as they used to when we or the generations before us were young. Wasn't it my grandmother and those in her generation that said, "it is important to stop and smell the roses."

4

PREVENTION

There are many things that we as adults can do to prevent early sexual experiences among our youth.

Before we begin a discussion on how we can change the emerging sexual trends among our youth, let's sum up what we have talked about so far. Let's start by looking at a compilation of our national statistics.

❋ 52% of High School students nationwide reported having sexual intercourse. This is down from the 1990's when it was 55%.

❋ 12% of these students reported having sexual intercourse before entering High School.

❋ 7.9% of these students reported having oral sex before entering High School.

❋ 1/3 of these students reported using NO PROTECTION.

❉ 1/4 of these students reported having had 4 or more sexual partners.

❉ 23.3% drank alcohol or used drugs prior to their last sexual experience.

Adults in our society often wonder how they can prevent our youth from engaging in sex at an early age and if they are already engaging in sexual activity what is the best mode of intervention. In this chapter we will focus on prevention. In the chapter that follows we will spend time looking at ways to intervene. Parents in particular are concerned about the sexual pressures their teens are facing. Most importantly, we need to begin to better communicate with our youth about sex. I cannot stress how imperative it is for parents to *talk* to their child about sex. It may surprise parents to know how much influence they actually have on their children regarding this topic. Kids report that they most frequently talk to their friends regarding sex. However, discussion with their parents is a close second. Take a look at the statistics below.

WHO DO TEENS TALK TO MOST OFTEN ABOUT SEX AND SEXUAL RELATIONSHIPS?

Friends	62%
Parents	41%
Brothers and sisters	28%
Teachers or the school nurse	12%
A religious person such as a minister, priest or rabbi	12%

Interestingly, teens will talk more often to their parents about sexual intercourse if they are actually having it. They are much less likely to talk with their parents about oral sex whether they are having it or not. The topic of oral sex is something they are much more likely to talk to their friends about. For most kids, this seems to be more embarrassing of a topic. The good news is that when it comes to sex education, teens report that they receive most of their information from their parents. Take a look at some of these statistics below:

WHO DO TEENS RECEIVE SEX EDUCATION FROM?

Parents	70%
Friends	53%
Teachers, the school counselor or nurse	53%
TV shows or movies	51%
Boyfriends, girlfriends or partners	37%
Magazines	34%
Brothers and sisters	26%
The Internet	19%

The topic of sexual education should start at an early age and progress through the child's various developmental stages. Most parents do this without even realizing it. A parent's first discussion about sex is usually with a young child when they are learning about their body parts and curious about everyone else's body parts. Parents make up names for various body parts when their child is young and a discussion tends to follow. Kids like to announce to people things like "poop is coming out of my bum bum" or "a ball hit me in my ding dong." Sometimes kids will just come right out and announce to their kindergarten class that "boys have a penis and girls have a vagina."

In the first two examples, we see that children are not using proper names to describe their private parts. Most parents assign cute or creative names for their child's various body parts because they think it is sweet or endearing. Others do it because this is what their parents called their body parts when they were little. Still others do it because they are embarrassed to use proper names. Although it seems to be the norm in our society to assign cute and creative names to body parts, several doctors encourage parents to use proper names when educating their children about anatomy. This is to avoid confusion among children who often will talk about their body parts with others especially at a young age when they just learned what they are called. (In case anyone is wondering, this type of discussion is developmentally appropriate and usually occurs when the child is around 4-5 years of age).

As a child becomes older and moves into a different phase of development, a different discussion regarding sex may occur. For example, a discussion about how babies are made may come up. This seems to be the 'kiss of death' question for most parents. For those of you that dread this question think about the questions that often follow once your child knows how babies are made. For example, be prepared for questions like: (1) Can people have sex if they are not married?" (2) "Why do people have sex if they don't want to make a baby?" (3) "What is birth control?" and (4) "What is a wet dream?"

Our children will undoubtedly ask about sex because they are hearing about sex from a variety of different sources. They hear about it from their friends and they hear about it in the music they listen to. They read about it in magazines and in books. They see it on television and in the movies they watch. In addition, they are easily able to access information about sex from the internet at any moment in time with a few typed words and a click of a button. Our youth are inundated with varying messages about sex that are usually unfiltered and unapproved by parents. Therefore, I strongly encourage parents to take the time to talk with their own children about sex. If you don't talk to them, their friends, their music, the media, and/or the internet will become their educators.

To illustrate this point, I would like to share a funny (or horrifying depending on how you want to look at it) story with you. One day I was at my son's preschool picking him up at the end of the day. When he got into the car, he proceeded to tell me what happened at lunchtime. He was sitting outside at the picnic tables with his little friends, when one of the girls in his class announced that her parents like to wrestle. One of the kids asked for clarification, "You're parents wrestle with each other?" The little girl answered, "yes." She then told them that in the morning she went into her parent's master bathroom to brush her teeth. When looking into the mirror, she saw her dad jumping up and down on her mom on their bed. She decided to stop brushing her teeth and enter their bedroom. She admitted that she was a little bit frightened at first because she thought that her daddy was being "too rough" with her mommy in their wrestling match. She told her little friends that her mommy and daddy were making cool wrestling sounds. She reported that they said things like "uh uh" and "ooo yeah." They even grunted at each other like "real wrestlers." When she entered their bedroom and said "daddy, stop being so rough with mommy, she doesn't like to wrestle," her mom replied, "it's o.k. honey, go back to your room, we are trying to make you a baby brother or sister."

When adults talk to children about sex, it is important that they speak to their child's age and maturity level. Be thoughtful about how you answer their questions. The example above is a good one. Although, these parents reassured their child that nothing was wrong and they spoke to her in a way that she could understand, they gave her a lot of information that she may have not been ready to hear. At the very least, their response could trigger several additional questions such as "What do you mean you are making a baby?" and/or "How are babies made?" Parents have to be prepared to answer these types of questions especially when they set themselves up for them.

Think about what you want to say to your child before you say it. This is most important because kids don't want to find out that their parents have lied to them. Therefore, a quick sugar coated response may not be ideal. A good friend of mine faced a problem with her daughter because her daughter thought she lied to her about something very important. My friend's highly intelligent 7 year old daughter came home from school one day very upset with her mother. When asked by her mother why she was so upset, the girl replied "Mommy, you lied to me!" She proceeded to tell her about a conversation she had at school with her second grade friends on the playground. They were all talking about how babies are born. One girl said, "they are pooped out." A boy corrected her and said, "No, they come out of your mom's vagina." When she said to her friends, "You are both wrong, they come out of your mommy's tummy" they all laughed at her. They said to her "No, that is where babies grow, but not where they come out from."

As the mother listened to her dauther tell this story, she was stunned. First, she could not believe that this was the topic of a second grade lunch hour. Second, she was not sure how to answer her daughter. She wanted to think this through and come up with the appropriate response, but she knew she did not have much time to respond. Her daughter was upset and wanted some answers. Clearly, the girl was not correct when she said "babies are pooped out" and even though the boy's answer was correct in several cases, it was not true in her daughter's case.

My friend decided to share with her daughter the facts. She explained to her that some babies come out of a mommy's vagina, but others do not when they are delivered via a Cesarean section (c-section). An explanation of what a c-section is and why it might be performed was not what she had planned for with her daughter at this young age.   However, she felt good about talking with her daughter openly and honestly and thus clearing up the fact that she did not "lie" to her. Her daughter asked to see her mother's scar. She was curious to see what part of her mother's body she actually came out of. When the mother showed the scar to her daughter, her daughter said, "Mommy, I think you are confused." She then stated, "Your stomach is higher than that scar; I think that is closer to your vagina!" Kids are smart! This is a good example of why doctors often recommend that we use proper names for our body parts. It causes less confusion. Kids often know more than adults give them credit for. Remember this the next time to talk to your kids about sex.

Sex is not the only thing that we should be talking to our children about starting at a young age. It is important to talk to them about relationships. Most people believe that this should be the first topic of discussion even before entering the topic of sex. Start by discussing how individuals treat one another when they care about someone. Hopefully you can reference models in your own home or in your own life. Give specific examples of how certain family members show love and respect toward other family members. Talk about holding hands and kissing. Talk about gestures of love and care. These gestures can be as simple as supporting the person by coming to their school performance or by hugging them when they are feeling sad.

If you don't have any role models in your own home who offer love and support, give examples of others who offer this to people they don't even know. For example, you can talk about how people in our country have recently shown love and support for the people in Haiti following their natural disaster. Donations of money, clothing, and medical supplies are all illustrations of caring for the needs of the Haitan people. Don't be afraid to use yourself as an example when talking to your children. Sometimes this is the best example you can give because your children directly relate to you. Point out what *you* have done for your child that illustrates your love for him/her. Also use yourself as an example to talk about the different kinds of relationships that people have with one another. Explain how loving your brother is very different than loving you're your friend or boyfriend. Do not assume that kids know the difference. Think about kids for example, who at a very young age say they want to marry their mother or father. They have no idea that this is not appropriate. It is not until parents inform them that they cannot marry their mother or father that they learn and understand this.

When educating our youth on the different kinds of relationships they will experience in their lives, it is important to talk about which ones may include sex. It is also important to educate them on which ones should NEVER include sex. I work with a lot of sexual assault victims in my private practice. It is not uncommon for an individual to come into my office telling me that they do not believe they were sexually abused even though they were molested by a family member, teacher or priest. In their minds, they consented and found the sexual encounters to be pleasurable; therefore, they saw the relationship as a "love relationship" and non-abusive.

One of my patients came into treatment after a 2 year sexual relationship with her rabbi because she realized when talking with her friends that this was not "normal." She just assumed that he did this with everyone during his private religious tutoring sessions. Another patient had no idea that it was not appropriate for her chiropractor to give her a vaginal exam at each weekly appointment. If you ever hear about a situation like this with your child or someone else's child, it is something that you should report to Child Protective Services (CPS) or to the police. Even if you are NOT a mandated reporter, a report can be made to the proper authorities in order to prevent further abuse and keep your child safe. Mandated reporters include mental health workers, teachers, child-care professionals, and almost anyone else that works with children. However, like I said, anyone can make a report.

Most parents beleive that they need some form of proof in order to make a report. They worry that the authorities will not believe them if they report abuse without it. To file a report, you should have some sort of *suspicion* that abuse is occurring. Proof is *not* necessary. You are not a detective and it is not your job to find proof of abuse. CPS and the police join forces and work together to investigate these types of crimes. Often reports are not filed. This is often due to a fear of getting involved. Many parents, neighbors, and friends are concerned that if they make a report, there will be some sort of reprecussion to them. Therefore, anonymous reports are allowed and often accepted by CPS. If you are uncertain as to whether or not you should be filing a report, you can make what is called a "screening call" to CPS. This is where you call a CPS worker, explain your concern for possible abuse, and ask them if a report should or should not be filed. They will direct you to do the right thing according to the situation.

Due to the potential for abuse in our society and the lack of understanding that many of our children have about what is and what is not appropriate sexual contact with varying people in their lives, it is important to talk to them about different kinds of relationships. As noted above, kids ask questions early on about all kinds of different relationships. At younger ages more now than ever before, they are asking about marriage, divorce, and separation. They will playfully tease their friends about who they think will marry who. They even pair themselves up with someone in their class and sing songs like "Susy and Johnny sittin in a tree, KISSING ... ." (Some things I guess will never change).

As older children, they will become more curious and ask questions about why one person in a marriage is older and why one is younger; why one is black and why one is white, why one is Jewish and why one is Christian, and why both people are the same sex instead of opposite sexes. With the overwhelming information and confusion they often face about relationships they may inform you that they will never get married and proceed to tell you why. Most give the reason that it is just too complicated. This opens the door for a great conversation that parents can have with their children about the complexities of relationships and why they should take marriage seriously.

Most kids are very aware, especially teenagers that 50% of marriages end in divorce. They simply need to look around their classroom and do a survey in their head to confirm this number. How you talk about these topics and answer all of these questions will shape your child's belief systems and views on some very loaded topics in our society. I cannot stress enough the importance of being thoughtful and careful about what you say. Take the time to think about what you want to say and what message you want to give to your child. Obviously, different individuals have different views about these things. Your children will encounter different viewpoints on these topics from their friends, teachers, neighbors, spiritual leaders, bosses, coaches, etc. Teach them first what you believe. Then help them learn how to handle the differing viewpoints and belief systems of their peers. What should and should they not say to others when their views differ.

I am a strong advocate of the acceptance of others and teaching our children how to agree to disagree. What we say to our children shapes their belief systems. We are their role models. Being a role model is a big job with a lot of responsibility. Do not underestimate how impactful you are on your child with what you do and what you say. I have been spending a lot of time in this chapter talking about the importance of communication with your children about sex and relationships. I would like to make a cautionary note to parents that when this communication occurs, it is important to remain in the parent role. Several parents unintentionally cross a boundary and talk to their child as if he/she is their friend. Your kids need you to be their parent, not their friend. This is especially true since some of the questions they may have for you are anxiety provoking for them. Therefore, they need a parent to calm their fears and help them to feel safe.

Recently, my colleague's 5 year old son asked her a lot of questions about why so many of his friends had divorced parents. She asked him if he knew what that word meant. He said "it's when a mom and dad don't live together in the same home." Her 8 year old son said, "And it means they are not married anymore." It brought up a discussion between them as to why parents get divorced. Her kids wanted to know. Most kids learn about divorce from their friends. Remember the statistic listed above? Half of their classmates are living in two separate homes due to their parents being either separated or divorced. Therefore, it is bound to come up in conversation.

Discussions like this can sometimes be anxiety provoking for kids because they worry that their own parents may get a divorce one day since this has happened to some of their friends. Be prepared for your child to ask you if you would ever consider divorce. Also be prepared to assure your child that your relationship is stable and healthy and happy (if it truly is). If it is not, do not use your child as a sounding board for your marital problems. Your child is not your therapist. Unfortunately, several parents make the mistake of talking to their child in this way which blurs boundaries and is often very upsetting to them. For example, it is highly upsetting for them to learn that their mother hates their father or that their father is having an affair. It is even more upsetting and worrisome for them to learn that their parent is depressed and possibly suicidal over it.

Parents in my professional experience are almost always well meaning. They do not intentionally want to cause their children psychological distress. When they cross this boundary with their children, they often see it as a way to develop an open and honest relationship with them. Their intent is almost always to become closer with their child through the sharing of personal information. Although this is not a bad theory when engaging in this type of communication with another adult, it is definitely the wrong thing to do with a child. They are too young and not yet able to cope with the intensity of emotions that this may bring to them. In addition, remember how and what you communicate with your children is a model of how and what they will communicate with others. Therefore, having your own personal boundaries with your children in turn, teaches them how to have their own personal boundaries with others.

I encourage parents to begin discussing personal boundaries with their children when they first start seeing their children become interested in someone else. For example, you may notice that your child is holding someone else's hand at school, hugging the same person at the end of each day before getting into your car or making comments about how "hot" they think someone is in their math class. Talk to them about boundaries as well as what you value in a relationship and why. This may include the importance of love, trust, understanding, and respect. Sometimes kids don't understand the difference between being in love with someone and feeling "lust" for someone. Unfortunately, with sex becoming more casual and crude, our kids tend to talk more about "fucking" or "screwing" someone rather than "making love" to someone. If you communicate about things like this with your kid, then your kid will more communicate about things like this with their partner. The more open you are and less embarrassed you are about talking about sex, the more open and less embarrassed they will be in talking with their partner about sex. Do you see the pattern here?

My hope is that if a teen is contemplating sex with their partner, then they are mature enough to talk to their partner about their readiness, willingness, comfort level, and desire to engage in various sexual activities. I would much rather have them talk about these things first, instead of just jumping into sexual activity with no discussion at all. When action happens before words, someone inevitable gets hurt and has regrets.

I have spent a lot of time talking about the importance of being a role model for our youth. Kids watch adult behavior and look to us for guidance all the time. Notice I said they **LOOK** to us for guidance. Most kids don't ask for guidance from their parents or other important adult role models in their lives unless they come from a family that is very communicative and open. However, just because they don't ask for guidance, does not mean that they do not **OBSERVE** what the adults are doing around them. For example, I have had several kids tell me about e-mails, texts, etc. they see sent between parents or one of their parents who is having an affair. If you are engaging in behaviors that include sexting and/or sex messaging there is a very high probability that your child is aware of it. I cannot tell you how many kids have shared with me stories about reading e-mails, online chats, and text messages that are sent between adults, which in the child's mind are incriminating. One of my patients found over 100 text messages between her father and his mistress. When the nude photos started being exchanged between them, she confronted him, and told her mother about his affair.

Kids are computer savvy. Many of them know how to hack into their parents private computer files and often do so to learn more about them. They hack past the parental controls on their own computers so they can visit whatever site they would like to visit without their parent's knowledge. Knowing that this occurs is even more reason to be the ones to talk with your children about sex and relationships. Your kids are more technologically advanced than you are. This is particularly true if they are catching you in the act. One girl told me at a school assembly last year that she caught her mother and father sending dirty text messages back and forth which said "What do you need right now?" The response "Cock." Interestingly, the same girl has been sending similar text messages to her boyfriend. Who do you think she learned this from?

This is not the only way we are role modeling negative behavior for our children. The media plays a role in this too, but not in the common way that you might think. Last weekend I was up really late at night. When I turned on the television, I saw an infomercial describing a new exercise craze. They were advertising pole dancing. The advertisement made a great argument for how a woman can lose weight and feel sexy at the same time. If she ordered this exercise package, she would receive in the mail, a pole (that is easily assembled in a common living area), and an instructional video to get started.

I didn't know if I should laugh or cry when I was watching this infomercial. All I could think about were all the young children who would soon be watching their mothers as they pole danced in the family room next to their dollhouses and lego sets. Surely, the mothers engaging in this exercise routine would not be thinking about the consequences of this modeling behavior, but instead about "shaping their abs and feeling sexy at the same time." However, this might change quickly for them when they get the call from their daughter's school informing them that she has been imitating her mother's fitness program on the flag pole located in the middle of the school for all her friends and teachers to see.

Since we have spent a lot of time so far in this chapter talking about the importance of communication with our youth, I think it is highly important to talk about how to have positive and healthy discussions with them. Most child experts will guide parents to always be open and honest and to always be a good listener when talking with children. What they don't say is how hard that can often be especially when the child is your own and when the topic is a tough one like sex. Maybe, like most parents, you are embarrassed by your 'old school' attitude and lack of knowledge of the changing sexual times. Maybe you don't want to sound prudish, naïve or foolish. In addition, you don't want to come off as highly critical, rude or oblivious. So where do you start? Start where your child is at.

Debra Haffner, author of a book called, *From Diapers to Dating*, says parents should take advantage of everyday "teachable moments." This means as mentioned earlier, that three year olds should have proper names for body parts and five year olds should know on a basic level where babies come from. Haffner does believe however, that parents should not give their young children more information than is appropriate or asked for, but should always answer their questions. Parents used to give "the birds and the bees talk" to their children at a certain age. Although this talk does promote education and communication, most professionals say that it is better to inform your kids along the way, instead of in one long sitting. In other words, do not have a 3 hour long talk with your child about sex, but rather several 'mini' talks when the timing seems right. Professionals agree with Haffner's "teachable moments" theory.

By the time your child reaches adolescents, they think they "know it all" and they will surely tell you that they do. However, this is not necessarily the case. If your child swears they *know everything*, and does not need to talk to you about anything; then simply tell him/her that you are glad they are so well informed, but now you want to share what you know with them. Try to do this when you are with your child alone as it prompts attentiveness and less embarrassment. For example, try having this discussion when in the car on the way to soccer practice or a piano lesson. The car is often a great place to talk to your child because there is less of chance for them to escape the conversation. Ask what he/she thinks about the sexual lyrics in their favorite song, the sexual images seen so often in the media, and what kids are doing at parties these days. Don't be afraid to focus on different things according to your child's age, gender, and maturity level.

We have already discussed varying topics due to age and maturity level; let's focus on varying topics due to gender. When talking to girls, the following things are important to discuss with them. The list below does not always come naturally to a girl. In fact, many of the items on the list below need to be taught. First, it is important to teach girls how to be assertive. They should be able to assertively tell their partner what they want and what they do not want in the relationship. This in part will include sex and intimacy. They may need some help understanding if and what they are ready for sexually. Therefore, it is helpful to talk to girls about the complexities of sex.

Most girls only think about how sex will change the relationship in a physical way. They do not think about or realize that it will change the relationship emotionally as well. We want our girls to be able to state very clearly to their partner what they are and what they are not comfortable doing sexually. Their comfort level can range from anything like holding hands and kissing to oral sex and sexual intercourse.

Girls should be educated that "NO MEANS NO." If they are not consenting to engaging in some form of sexual activity, then it is a sexual assault. It is helpful to teach girls how to say NO in creative ways. It is not that easy for them to always say NO. For example, if they love the other person and they don't want to disappoint them or hurt their feelings, it might be hard to say NO. Also, if boundaries are being pushed in a loving, gentle way that does not feel abusive to them, even though they do not want to go farther sexually, they might have difficulty saying NO. Therefore, simply guiding girls to just say NO does not always work. Sometimes it is helpful to script for them what they might say in different situations. For example, if the girl is in love with her partner and doesn't want to hurt or disappoint the one she loves, she might say, "I love you and because our relationship is so important and special to me, I want to wait." Or "I am not ready to have sex yet and I want to be so that when we do have sex it will be really special between us."

If the girl has an action plan, she will feel much more confident in the situation and empowered by her words.

There is a possibility that saying no, either directly or more indirectly will not work. This brings me to the second thing that we need to teach our girls. We need to teach them what to do if someone comes on too strong and will not take NO for an answer. Both verbal and physical responses are helpful for a girl to have in a her 'tool box.' One way for girls to learn several different tools (ways that they can intervene) is by taking a self-defense class. These classes usually begin by focusing on verbal interventions. They talk about how a girl can firmly tell someone to stop what they are doing as well as how to get other people's attention if they are in trouble. For example, yelling "fire" when being attacked works really well in a public place even if there are not many people around. This works much better then yelling "help." Research shows that people react when they hear the word "fire" almost immediately. Unfortunately, this is not always true when they hear the word "help."

Along with teaching girls how to intervene verbally, self-defense classes teach girls how to intervene physically. It is important for girls to know how to physically defend themselves if they are under attack. The classes provide good physical defense tools. For example, they will teach girls that the best place to strike a person on the face (if they are trying to get away from their attacker) is either a hit to the nose or a gauging of the eyes. The best place to strike a person on their lower body is a hit to the knee or if the person is male, a hit to the groin. Lastly, a self-defense class will also teach girls how to avoid or reduce the risk of being attacked by an acquaintance or stranger.

Below are 9 tips every girl or woman should know. These tips could save a woman's life and keep her from harm. This is a list that a friend of mine recently sent to me via e-mail. She was given this list at the self-defense class she attended this year.

1. Tip from Tae Kwon Do: The elbow is the strongest point on your body. If you are close enough to use it, do!

2. Learned this from a tourist guide in New Orleans. If a robber asks for your wallet and/or purse, DO NOT HAND IT TO HIM. Instead, toss it away from you....chances are that he is more interested in your wallet and/or purse than you, and he will go for the wallet/purse. RUN LIKE MAD IN THE OTHER DIRECTION!

3. If you are ever thrown into the trunk of a car, kick out the back tail lights and stick your arm out the hole and start waving like crazy. The driver won't see you, but everybody else will. This has saved lives.

4. Women have a tendency to get into their cars after shopping, eating, working, etc., and just sit (doing their checkbook, or making a list, etc.) DON'T DO THIS! The predator will be watching you, and this is the perfect opportunity for him to get in on the passenger side, put a gun to your head, and tell you where to go. AS SOON AS YOU GET INTO YOUR CAR, LOCK THE DOORS AND LEAVE. AND... If someone is in the car with a gun to your head DO NOT DRIVE OFF, repeat: DO NOT DRIVE OFF! Instead gun the engine and speed into anything, wrecking the car. Your Air Bag will most likely save you. If the person is in the back seat they will get the worst of it. As soon as the car crashes, get out of the car and run. It is better than having them find your body in a remote location.

5. A few notes about getting into your car in a parking lot or parking garage: A) Be aware: look around you, look into your car, at the passenger side floor, and in the back seat. B) If you are parked next to a big van, enter your car from the passenger door. Most serial killers attack their victims by pulling them into their vans while the women are attempting to get into their cars. C) Look at the car parked on the driver's side of your vehicle, and the passenger side. If a male is sitting alone in the seat nearest your car, you may want to walk back into the mall, or work, and get a guard/policeman to walk you back out. IT IS ALWAYS BETTER TO BE SAFE THAN SORRY. (And better paranoid than dead.) Another tip I was recently given concerning cars, if you are ever locked into a car and the keys are in the ignition obviously drive that van away from there... fast! BUT if no keys are in the ignition jam it with something like a bobby pin (break it in there) or even a wad of chewing gum... remember, leaving the primary location is the worst situation possible, if he cant start his van... he is going to have a much harder time transporting you.

6. ALWAYS take the elevator instead of the stairs. (Stairwells are horrible places to be alone and the perfect crime spot. This is especially true at NIGHT!)

7. If the predator has a gun and you are not under his control, ALWAYS RUN! The predator will only hit you (a running target) 4 in 100 times; And even then, it most likely WILL NOT be a vital organ. RUN, pref-

erably, in a zig -zag pattern! (This was confirmed in the K.C. Star)

8. As women, we are always trying to be sympathetic: STOP! It may get you raped or killed. Ted Bundy, the serial killer, was a good-looking, well educated man, who ALWAYS played on the sympathies of unsuspecting women. He walked with a cane or a limp, and often asked "for help" into his vehicle or with his vehicle, which is when he abducted his next victim.

9. Another Safety Point: Someone just told me that her friend heard a crying baby on her porch the night before last, and she called the police because it was late and she thought it was weird. The police told her "Whatever you do, DO NOT open the door." The lady then said that it sounded like the baby had crawled near a window, and she was worried that it would crawl to the street and get run over. The policeman said, "We already have a unit on the way, whatever you do, DO NOT open the door." He told her that they think a serial killer has a baby's cry recorded and uses it to coax women out of their homes thinking that someone dropped off a baby. He said they have not verified it, but have had several calls by women saying that they hear baby's cries outside their doors when they're home alone at night.

One thing that the tips above do not inform girls about is that there is a high correlation between substance abuse and sexual assault. We have already talked about the correlation between the two above in regards to a person's increasedwillingness to engage in sexual activity when intoxicated. However, we have not yet discussed the fact that a girl is at much higher risk of sexual assault if either she or her partner is intoxicated.

The connection between substance abuse and sexual assault is the third thing that we should educate our girls about. For example, we need to talk to our girls about utilizing "the buddy system." This is particularly true if they are ever at a party where people are drinking and/or doing drugs. Does anyone remember the "buddy system" from when we were in elementary school? It is a system most schools still use today nationwide in order to assure the safety of our children. The theory behind it is that we are safer when in pairs of two than when we are alone. By pairing people up together, individuals are less likely to get lost or harmed. This is true for teenagers and adults alike.

If our teenage girls are at a party, it is better to have a friend or friends looking out for them. Our teenage girls tend to be very good about doing this. Most of the girls that I talk to make sure that they utilize this system. They also make sure that they never leave their drink (even if it is just water) unattended because someone could slip something into it (i.e., a date rape drug). Girls want to be safe and obviously do not want to be harmed in anyway. Therefore, teaching them precautionary measures is incredibly important.

It is also important for parents to set rules for their daughters that make sense for them and at the same time keep them safe. In other words, parents should set rules around safety planning. This is a proactive way to reduce the possibility of harm if your daughter finds herself in a dangerous situation. For example, if your daughter is at a party where she consumes alcohol, can she call you if she needs a ride home? Can she come to you with questions about sex? Can she ask for your help to get on birth control? Tell your daughter what your limits are as parents and be consistent with following through with the limits that you set. This is an incredibly important thing for parents to abide by. Nothing is worse than a parent who sets a clear and consistent limit and then does not follow through with that limit. If you do not follow through, you are basically telling your child that you cannot be trusted and that you are not true to your word. Isn't this the definition of integrity? You are better off not setting the limit in the first place then setting it and not following through with it. At least this way, your kids will trust you and beleive what you say. We will talk more about this later in this chapter.

Let's move on to some specific things that we can teach our boys. First and foremost, I believe we need to teach our boys to be both respectful and understanding that a girl may not be ready for sex even if she is "going along with it." Fortunately, most boys do respect and honor the word NO! However, sometimes, the word NO is not spoken verbally. Instead girls show non-verbal signs that they may not be ready to engage in sexual activity. Clearly, it is preferable for a girl to verbally voice her thoughts on this matter, but this is not always the case. Therefore, it is helpful to teach our boys to ask a girl what she wants and what she is comfortable with since so many of them have a hard time expressing this verbally.

If boys can get in the routine of having an open communication about what the girl is comfortable with regarding sex and intimacy than half the battle is fought. Several boys talk to me about the fact that girls "confuse" them. They say that a girls might tell them that they don't want to have sex initially, but then they sit on their laps and rub up against them acting as if they do. They will even go as far as bringing them into a bedroom, locking the door behind them, and then aggressively coming onto them. Many boys in these situations (which is more common than you might think), believe that the girl has changed her mind from what she said earlier. And why wouldn't they think so? After all, their actions are speaking much louder than their words. In these situations, boys then become more sexually aggressive themselves and when they "cross a line" (according to the girl), the girl gets angry and reiterates that she is uncomfortable with "going that far." To a boys dismay, the girl may even accuse him of attacking her. In some cases this is exactly what may have occurred, however, in others it is not. Many of you reading this might think that this is unfair and in some cases it may be. However, the reality of the matter is that a girl's word does matter. NO MEANS NO - Period!!!

The girl in the example above, may be labeled by many as a "tease." With our new sexual revolution in full swing, we are seeing girls "teasing" boys in much more sexually advanced and aggressive ways. Therefore, I will stress again the importance of needing to teach boys to ask their partner questions about their desire, comfort, and intent to engage in sexual activity with them. Boys should ask these questions in a respectful way each time they are with a girl, especially if they are getting mixed messages from her.

I often encourage boys when they are getting mixed messages from girls to point out the discrepancy to the girl. Many of the boys I have talked to have had great success in doing this with girls. It almost always gives them immediate clarification and stops the girl from sending the mixed messages in the future. A lot of times girls are unaware that they are sending these contradictory messages. They need this awareness in order to stop doing it. When mixed messages are present, it places both boys and girls at greater risk for sexual encounters that are unwanted and unhealthy. When talking to the boys about this, give examples of how they can approach girls to have conversations about sex. Similarly to girls, boys often need scripting. It is not always easy for them to talk about these types of things. Therefore, they may need help as to what they should say and when they should say it. For example, it is probably not the best timing or place to have a conversation about sex in the cafeteria at school with hundreds of kids around. It is also not ideal to have the conversation over Facebook or though text messaging. Face to face conversations allow for a more intimate discussion on what should be an intimate topic.

One of the things that is not taught to boys nearly enough is that it is "o.k." for them to say NO to sex. We do not even consider the fact that boys may not be ready to have sex, however, we need to. For centuries, it has been said that boys "are always ready." Girls are taught that boys "only have one thing on their minds." However, this is not always the case. Many boys are NOT ALWAYS ready and are not necessarily "making the first move" anymore. This is particularly true with the emerging trend of girls in our society becoming more sexually aggressive and asserting themselves to boys in highly sexual ways. With this shift, they are often the ones to make the first move and assume that boys will naturally be happy participants with whatever they desire.

More boys now than ever before are actually distraught over the fact that they are not ready for sex. They do not readily admit this to anyone though because they are afraid of being seen as a "whimp." Therefore, they engage in sexual activity despite that fact that they are not ready. It is incredibly important for us to dispel the myth that "boys were born ready" to have sex and to talk to them about peer pressure. This is another opportunity for adults to help boys script what they might say to a girl who is coming on to them too strong.

For most parents with girls, this notion may seem far-fetched. A girl coming on too strong to a guy is not something that commonly occurred in the past, but is happening more and more today. If you don't believe this talk to parents of boys. Several of them have shared stories with me about catching a girl climbing into their son's bedroom window in the middle of the night. In addition, girls are taking off their own shirts, sitting on a boys lap half naked, and then proceeding to make out with them in front of all their friends. We need to help boys prepare for these types of situations when they do not want to be sexually active. *On a side note, has anyone seen the video series "Girls Gone Wild?" Maybe you should not answer that question out loud. It is a video series that grossed millions of dollars as it illustrates topless women partying and acting sexually promiscuous for the whole world to see. In any case, it is no wonder why our girls are acting this way. Once again we see that they have plenty of adult role models to show them the way. O.K., back to our boys.

It is particularly hard for boys to refuse what girls are offering to them sexually especially when their friends are around or watching. One of the reasons that boys are often not ready to have sex is the fact that they are uneducated about it. Remember it is the boy that is supposed to be experienced. It is the boy who is supposed to have "all the moves" and take control of the situation. If the boy has no idea of what he is doing, it is scary and intimidating for him. He certainly does not want to embarrass himself and "ruin his reputation."

I worked with a teen boy several years ago that came into my office absolutely petrified about his weekend plans with his girlfriend of 2 years. He was 17 years old at the time and his girlfriend announced to him that she was ready to have sex. She wanted to have sex over the weekend when the boy's parents had planned to be out of town. She assumed that he would be excited because in her mind "he waited 2 years for her to be ready." However, he was not excited at all. In fact, he was petrified. He was not ready to have sex. He was scared that it would change things in their relationship. Many of his friends who already were having sex informed him that it makes girls much more "dependent and clingy." He liked the way things were with his girlfriend and did not want things to change because of sex. The boy was also completely "freaked out" that if they did have sex, he would do something "wrong" and completely humiliate himself. When I asked him what he was afraid he would do wrong, he replied, "what if I put it in the wrong hole?" He said that his concern was if the room was dark, he would not be able to see what he was doing.

This particular boy exudes confidence on a daily basis. Most people who knew him would probably be surprised to know what his thoughts were about sex. He was the quarterback on his high school football team, the stereotypical good looking jock, and a great student. He had the reputation of being the "most popular boy" at school and as we old folks would say "a great catch." It was scary for him to think that this somehow could be all thrown away if he did not perform well. People were used to him performing well. He was used to him performing well. This was not that simple for him and he had nobody to talk to about it except for me. His parents were going through a terrible divorce which is why he was in counseling. He wished he could talk to his dad, but his dad was never around. His mother was always "emotional" and bad mouthing "men in general." Obviously, this was painful to hear from his own mother's mouth since he himself was soon to be a man. In any case, he was grateful to discuss his worries with a therapist.

Despite what most of us think, boys need adults to talk to about the complexities of relationships and sex. This may be particularly true since boys from the beginning of time have been taught how to get what they want and to "go for it" when it comes to girls. Conversely, girls are expected to be the "gatekeepers." This objectifying mentality speaks to the failure by adults in our society to instill in boys the kind of empathy that would translate into a greater degree of caring in their sexual relationships. Therefore, this is another area of teaching for our boys.

According to the research done by author, Sharlene Azam who wrote the book, *Oral Sex is the Next Goodnight Kiss*, 8th and 9th grade boys, who relentlessly pursued girls at school, eventually got what they wanted. After 3 hours of being followed around school being told "You're so beautiful, why don't you give me a blow job," the girls gave in. Research also showed that although parents of the boys were surprised to find out their sons were having oral sex at school, they were unwilling to fault them. Most of the parents believed that it was the girl's responsibility because "boys will be boys." In addition, the parents of the girls were upset and embarrassed by their behavior but did not see it as cause for alarm because "kids experiment with sex all the time."

So if we know that kids will experiment with sex, then how can we intervene as adults in our society to make sure that they are being safe and making good choices for themselves and their partners? Communication about relationships and sex is half the battle. It is in fact what will prevent this type of early experimentation from happening in the first place. However, if communication ends up not being enough, then we have to move into the intervention phase. In the next chapter, we will explore this phase in great detail.

5

INTERVENTION

Prevention and intervention often go hand in hand.

We make attempts to prevent a situation from occurring, while at the same time preparing to intervene if necessary. The first step in preparing for an intervention is acquiring knowledge about the situation. Parent can do this by monitoring what is happening in their child's life. The best way to find out what is happening in your child's life is to ask him/her. Therefore, communication will remain present in intervention phase.

There is the possibility that when you attempt communication with your child, he/she will not talk to you. If this occurs try finding out some information about your child on your own. I do not recommend talking to his/her friends, snooping around their room, and/or looking through their private belongings. Your child does have a right to some privacy. However, there are many things that you can do that would not invade his/her privacy. For example, try typing in their screen name, e-mail address or cell phone number into Google and see what pops up. You may find your son or daughter's picture and tons of should be private information about them listed on popular sites like MySpace and facebook.com. They may also be on several less popular sites such as hotornot.com, buddypic.com, facebattle.com, and facethejury.com. What you find can be the opening of a conversation with them. Remember not to attack them the instant you initiate a conversation with them even if you are unhappy with what you have found. If you are critical and blameful, your child will inevitably shut down and all hopes of a conversation will be lost. This does not mean that you will praise them for the things that alarm you as a parent; it simply means that you will remain neutral in order to initiate an open and honest interchange.

Another way to monitor what your child is doing is by looking at your son or daughter's live journal or blog – if they have one. Most parents have no idea if their child has such a thing. If they are aware that they have one, they often do not read it. I am a very strong advocate of privacy as I mentioned just a few moments ago. Therefore, if a young person chooses to keep a private diary or journal handwritten under their bed, I guide parents not to read it. However, a live journal and/or blog is different. This is not under lock and key. In fact, it is the opposite. It is a public posting and there is nothing wrong with reading your child's entries if they are posting them on the internet for the whole world to see. A live journal or blog can be read by thousands of other people including individuals that do not know your child and have never met your child. Perhaps this is one of the main reasons if parents are not reading their child's live journal or blog, they should be.

Safety should always come first. How much personal information are your kids giving to complete strangers? Most parents are shocked to find that there is a lot of personal and private information being shared. Most of the time, kids are oblivious that this could be a safety concern. This is due to a lack of education on internet safety. Parents, teachers, coaches, clergy, and even police officers have made their concerns known about teens disclosing such an extensive amount of personal information to others on a public website. Due to these growing concerns, families, schools, community agencies, and religious organizations have begun to educate teens about internet saftey. Fortunately, this has resulted in teens being much more protective of their profiles. Several teens (66% according to Pew Research) choose to keep their profiles "private" so that only the people they accept as "friends" can view it.

I believe that with knowledge comes power. However, I also believe that with ignorance comes bliss. As a parent raising children in our society, you have to decide which motto you would like to stand behind. When it comes to a full understanding about the emerging sexual trends among our youth, I choose knowledge over ignorance. Therefore, I strongly encourage adults become knowledgeable about sex and the language circled around it when it comes to our youth. This is particularly helpful when a parent is trying to monitor their child's behavior. After all, it is much easier to monitor something when you know what you are looking for.

Kids have created a whole new language that is foreign to most adults in our society. It is a language based on abbreviations and slang terms. Many parents use a filtering program designed to alert them if their child is talking with their friends about a topic of concern (i.e., sex, pornography, violence, drugs, etc.) The program identifies these conversations by picking up on key term that would indicate a discussion on one of the topics listed above. These programs have proven successful for monitoring children's conversations. However, kids are smart and they know how to get around these filters. For example, your filters may pick up the word 'porn,' but do they catch the word 'pron?' which kids use instead to fake out the system. What about the word *paw*, short for "parents are watching" or *pos* for "parents over shoulder." At the back of this book, I have compiled a list of some words and abbreviations that your filters may not pick up. The meanings of these words and abbreviations are attached to them. (See Appendix B)

Parents also use other blocking systems on their computers. Probably the most popular are the ones that block certain websites such as pornography sites. However, it is important to consider that this does not assure full security from access to these sights. In fact, any teenager can tell you that online search engines are the best free porn sites ever. Take a look at Google Image Search for example. Go ahead, try it. Just type in anything remotely dirty and see what you get.

I know this all seems a little deflating especially to parents who have taken the precautions they thought were sufficient to prevent access to adult websites. So what can you do? Talk to your kids. Again we are back to communication. Remember the statistics listed above. The majority of children listen to their parents when they talk to them about sex. In addition, get your own copy of AOL Instant Messenger and put your kids' names on your buddy list. Read their profiles, you'll be surprised what you find in there.

It is important to note that your kids are not necessarily trying to hide *everything* from you. In fact, many of them report they wish they could have a closer relationship with their parents. Most of them think they cannot talk to their parents because their parents won't listen to them or because they will be misunderstood. It is important for parents to *try* to understand where their kids are coming from. You do not have to agree with what your child is doing. However, if you don't even know *what* they are doing, then there is no chance of intervention. At least if you are aware of what is happening in your child's life and you do not agree with some of the choices they are making, then you can talk to them about it. This may be the only chance you have to help them see things differently and change their behavior.

Often, parents don't get a lot of answers from their children because they are not asking them any questions. A

lot of kids are willing to share a whole lot more information with adults than adults think they will. It never ceases
to amaze me how open and honest kids usually are and I
don't mean only when I see them professionally. Have
you ever been in line at a Starbucks either in front or
behind two teenagers? They will talk about anything and
everything that is on their minds in that moment in time.
It does not seem to phase them that they are talking about
what used to be considered by most as very private topics
(i.e. sex) in front of several strangers in a very public
place. Frequently, I want to tap them on the shoulder and
say, "do you really want the whole line of Starbucks cus-
tomers to know about your sex life?" Kids in our society
today seem to care less about privacy and what others
think about them, then the generations of people who
lived before them. Therefore, it is an ideal time for
parents to ask *more* questions and try to get to know their
kids on a deeper level.

If you are highly concerned about your child's behavior
which places them at high risk (i.e., sneaking out of the
house, substance use, promiscuity, etc.) then your child
may need some form of therapeutic intervention.
Remember as parents you do not want to cross this line
yourself and try to become their therapist. Let me take the
time to reiterate this point once again. Just as we discussed earlier, you do not want to use your child as your
therapist and therefore, similarly, you do not want your
child to use you as their therapist. Instead, if you do have
concerns for your child because you believe he/she is

making some unhealthy and/or unsafe choices seek out a counselor for them to talk to as soon as possible.

Usually there is some underlying cause for a young person's acting out behavior. For example, the individual may be experiencing depression, anxiety, and/or post traumatic stress due to a trauma. Therapists can help with this and early intervention is a key component to success. Research shows that the sooner the child is in treatment, the higher the success rate. Another key component to successful treatment is the person's motivation and willingness to be in counseling. This usually is increased if the individual likes who they see. Therefore, it is important to find the right therapist for your child. Your child needs to feel comfortable opening up to his/her therapist. If he/she does not trust the therapist, then there will be greater resistance to change. A strong therapeutic alliance is often listed as the number reason for success in treatment, which is why I cannot reiterate enough the importance of finding a 'good fit' for your child.

If parents have entered the intervention phase, then it usually means whatever preventative measures they have taken thus far have not work. Often parents experience a lot of guilt and shame when this occurs. It is not productive for parents to blame themselves. I realize this is a lot easier said than done. However, it is highly important for parents to try not to fall into this trap. It is very frustrating for kids when their parents blame themselves and "feel sorry for themselves." Most teens view this as their parents throwing themselves a "pity party." This actually annoys teens because it makes the unresolved problems more about the parent and less about the them. Kids in trouble need our help and most of the time even if they don't admit it, they want our help. We need to keep them at the center of our attention. Therefore, I encourage parents to take care of themselves so they can better intervene with their children. Please see a list at the end of this book that describes ways you as a parent can take care of yourself so that you are better able to serve your child. (Appendix C).

Whether your child is in a high risk situation or a low risk situation, it is a good idea for parents to set limits with their children on the topics that they are concerned about. For example, if you are concerned that your child is spending too much time on the computer, then set limits on how much time they are allowed each day (this may vary from weekdays to weekends). If you are worried about what your child is doing on the computer, then set limits on where they can access the computer (i.e. in the general living room where it can be monitored) and what sites they can and cannot visit. Remember as mentioned earlier, if you are going to set a limit, you should plan on following through with the limit that you set. If you do not, you are sending your child a very clear message that you are not true to your word. Teenagers in particular have very little respect for parents that are inconsistent and untrustworthy. They very much prefer to have consistent boundaries and limits than no boundaries and limits at all.

To close, I want to acknowledge that every child and family situation is different. I would never suggest that this book unlocks all the mysteries and manifestations of the emerging sexual trends in our society. We have discussed in great length the important role that parents play in the lives of their children. We have focused on the importance of communication, limit setting and role modeling for our youth. I strongly believe that as a community, we can work together to build solid relationships with our children. With a strong relationship in place, it is hopeful that we can better guide our youth to make good, healthy decisions regarding sex and relationships. Identifying the many problems that our youth face and gaining a better understanding for them gives us the opportunity and privilege to help guide our youth in positive ways not only in regards to the topic of sex, but in all areas of their lives.

6

APPENDIX

APPENDIX A

NATIONAL COLLEGE STATISTICS

(Source: "The Sexual Victimization of College Women"; National Institute of Justice and the Bureau of Justice Statistics; December, 2000.). In the US, each academic year, for every 5000 female students, there are:

* ❊ 97 rapes by force or threat of force
* ❊ 80 attempted rapes by force or threat of force
* ❊ 121 rapes by coercion
* ❊ 146 sexual contacts with force or threat of force
* ❊ 149 sexual contacts by coercion
* ❊ 46.5% of those who experienced a completed rape defined it as rape
* ❊ 90% knew the offender

* 52% took place after midnight; 37% took place 6:00pm to midnight
* The majority of both on and off campus assaults occurred in the person's living quarters
* More sexual assaults occurred off campus than on campus
* Less than 5% of completed and attempted rapes were reported to the police 2/3 told someone but rarely a college official

DATA COLLECTED BY THE WISCONSIN COALITION AGAINST SEXUAL ASSAULT

* The most vulnerable population for campus rape are freshman girls during the first few months of school. Many of these girls were virgins before they were raped. (Neimark, Jill. Out of Bounds, the Truth About Athletes and Rape. Interactivetheater.org, 2000.)
* 1 out of 6 college women have been raped or have been the victim of an attempted rape during the past year. (Weitzman, E., DeJong, W., and Finn, P. Alcohol and Acquaintance Rape: Strategies to Protect Yourself and Each Other. The Higher Education Center for Alcohol and Other Drug Prevention. U.S. Department of Education, 1999.)
* 1 out of 15 male students raped or attempted to rape a woman during the past year. (Weitzman, E., DeJong, W., and Finn, P. Alcohol and Acquaintance Rape: Strategies to Protect Yourself and Each Other. The Higher Education Center for Alcohol and Other Drug Prevention. U.S. Department of Education, 1999.)

- 7 out of 10 rape or sexual assault victims knew their attacker. (Rennison, Calli M. Criminal Victimization 1998: Changes 1997-1998 with Trends 1993-1998. Bureau of Justice Statistics, U.S. Department of Justice, 1999.)
- 1/4 of all college-age rape victims blame themselves entirely for the attack. (Schwartz, M., Leggett, M. Bad Dates or Emotional Trauma- the Aftermath of Campus Sexual Assault. Violence Against Women, Vol. 5, No. 3, March, 1999.)
- Only 5% of undergraduate women reported their sexual assault to police. (Schwartz, M., Leggett, M. Bad Dates or Emotional Trauma- the Aftermath of Campus Sexual Assault. Violence Against Women, Vol. 5, No. 3, March, 1999.)
- 75% of male students and 55% of female students involved in date rape had been drinking or using drugs at the time. (Koss, M.P. 1998. Hidden Rape: Incident, Prevalence, and Descriptive Characteristics of Sexual Aggression and Victimization in a National Sample of College Students. Rape and Sexual Assault, Vol. II. edited by A.W. Burgess. New York: Garland Publishing Company.)
- 84% of men whose actions matched the legal definition of rape, said that what they did was definitely not rape. (Koss, M.P. 1998. Hidden Rape: Incident, Prevalence, and Descriptive Characteristics of Sexual Aggression and Victimization in a National Sample of College Students. Rape and Sexual Assault, Vol. II. edited by A.W. Burgess. New York: Garland Publishing Company.)

❈ Gang rapes on campus are most often perpetrated by men who participate in intensive male peer groups (such as fraternities or athletic teams) that foster rape supportive behaviors and attitudes. (Sexual Assault and Alcohol and Other Drug Use. The Higher Education Center for Alcohol and other Drug Prevention. U.S. Department of Education. June, 1998.)

APPENDIX B

TOP 25 INTERNET SLANG TERMS

ASL(R P)	Age Sex Location (Race / Picture)
BF / GF	Boyfriend / Girlfriend
BRB	Be Right Back
CD9	Code 9 - means parents are around
GNOC	Get Naked on Cam (webcam)
GTG	Got to Go
IDK	I don't know
(L)MIRL	(Lets) meet in real life
LOL	Laugh Out Loud
MorF	Male or Female
MOS	Mom Over Shoulder
NIFOC	Naked in Front of Computer
Noob	Newbie - often an insult to somebody who doesn't know much
NMU	Not much, you?
P911	Parent Emergency
PAW	Parents are Watching
PIR	Parent In Room
POS	Parent Over Shoulder
PRON	Porn
PRW	Parents Are Watching
S2R	Send To Receive (pictures)
TDTM	Talk Dirty To Me
Warez	Pirated Software
W/E	Whatever
WTF	What the Fuck?
DTF	Down to Fuck?

TOP INTERNET AND CHAT ACRONYMS

8	Oral Sex
1337	Elite –or- leet – or- L337
143	I Love You
182	I Hate You
1174	Nude Club
420	Marijuana
459	I love you
ADR	Address
AEAP	As Early As Possible
ALAP	As Late As Possible
ASL	Age/Sex/Location
CD9	Code 9 – it means parents are around
C-P	Sleepy
F2F	Face-to-Face
GNOC	Get Naked On Cam
GYPO	Get Your Pants Off
HAK	Hugs And Kisses
ILU	I Love You
IWSN	I Want Sex Now
J/O	Jerking Off
KOTL	Kiss On The Lips
KFY –or- K4Y	Kiss For You
KPC	Keeping Parents Clueless
LMIRL	Let's Meet In Real Life
MOOS	Member Of The Opposite Sex
MOSS	Member Of The Same Sex
MorF	Male or Female
MOS	Mom Over Shoulder
MPFB	My Personal F*** Buddy
NALOPKT	Not A Lot Of People Know That
NIFOC	Nude In Front Of The Computer
NMU	Not Much, You?
P911	Parent Alert
PAL	Parents Are Listening
PAW	Parents Are Watching
PIR	Parents In Room

POS	Parent Over Shoulder –or- Piece Of SH**
Pron	Porn
Q2C	Quick To Cum
RU/18	Are You Over 18?
RUMORF	Are You Male Or Female?
RUH	Are You Horny?
S2R	Send to Receive
SorG	Straight Or Gay
TDTM	Talk Dirty To Me
WTF	What The F***
WUF	Where You From
WYCM	Will You Call Me
WYRN	What's Your Real Name?
Zerg	To Gang Up On Someone
BRB	Be Right Back
BFF	Best Friends Forever
FUD	Fear, Uncertainty And Disinformation
OMG	Oh My God
TMI	Too Much Information
WYWH	Wish You Were Here
SWAK	Sealed With A Kiss
SITD	Still In The Dark

APPENDIX C

HOW TO TAKE CARE OF THE CARETAKER

EXERCISE:

1. Walk by yourself or with others
2. Go for a Jog
3. Go on a Hike
4. Take a Bike Ride
5. Attend a Yoga class
6. Attend an Exercise Class
7. Dance

SLEEP:

1. 8 hours of sleep is ideal and recommended by most doctors
2. If sleep deprived, naps during the day can help

RELAXATION AND LEISURE TIME:

1. Listen to Music
2. Take a long hot bubble bath
3. Get a facial, manicure, pedicure or massage

EXPRESSION:

1. Write (Journal, Poetry, Letters etc.)
2. Draw or Paint
3. Dance

SUPPORT:

1. Talk to friends or family members
2. Talk to a therapist
3. Find other parents that are going through something similar with their children and brainstorm what works and what doesn't work with teens in your community
4. Talk to a spiritual adviser